We stand at a critical moment in our nation's history. We need to encounter God and take action as the powers of darkness continue raging against the moral fabric of America. This book will stir your spirit to pray for revival and a spiritual awakening in our nation. A must-read!

—MIKE BICKLE
AUTHOR, *GROWING IN PRAYER* AND *PASSION FOR JESUS*
FOUNDER, INTERNATIONAL HOUSE OF PRAYER–KC

What a rich resource! Jennifer LeClaire has offered strong warning, resounding hope, and a clear path to revival by drawing on the insights of a wide variety of leaders, both past and present, as well her own heart—a heart obviously fully devoted to Jesus. She joins a rising chorus of prophetic voices crying out for a true modern-day reformation. Read and reread this book. It is much needed and wonderfully refreshing!

—R. LOREN SANDFORD
AUTHOR, *YES, THERE'S MORE*
PASTOR, NEW SONG CHURCH AND MINISTRIES

William Booth, an 1800s Methodist preacher and founder of The Salvation Army, stated, "I consider that the chief dangers which confront the coming century will be religion without the Holy Ghost, Christianity without Christ, forgiveness without repentance, salvation without regeneration, politics without God, and heaven without hell." How eerily prophetic and insightful his words seem to be for us today. Yet, in the midst of dark getting darker, the light of Christ is getting brighter. Jennifer LeClaire has refreshingly shed a spotlight on what the Lord is doing in and through many streams in the body of Christ. It only takes a few seeds to produce a great harvest and spark revival fires. Unconnected groups are spontaneously seeking the presence of the Lord through corporate times of worship, prayer, and fastedness. It's like a picture of many flickers of flames or candles across the land, yet when the Holy Spirit wind blows upon them, it will turn into one great fire of revival.

—DOUG STRINGER
FOUNDER AND PRESIDENT, SOMEBODY CARES AMERICA AND
SOMEBODY CARES INTERNATIONAL

Jennifer LeClaire speaks my heart as she calls for our repentance—without excuse and without compromise—and points us toward America's only hope: a national awakening. Your heart will be stirred as you read these pages. It's an urgent time in America, but it's not too late for divine intervention.

—DR. MICHAEL L. BROWN
AUTHOR, FOUNDER, AND PRESIDENT OF FIRE SCHOOL OF
MINISTRY, AND HOST OF THE *LINE OF FIRE*

Jennifer LeClaire weaves a tapestry through the voices of many of God's servants that something very big is coming. Get ready! We stand on the brink of the greatest move of God the world has ever seen, which will result in the greatest harvest of souls and usher in the return of the King. May this book stir your heart to pray and to position yourself so that you can be actively involved in the next move of God.

—DR. RODNEY M. HOWARD-BROWNE
PRESIDENT AND FOUNDER OF REVIVAL MINISTRIES INTERNATIONAL
FOUNDING PASTOR OF THE RIVER @ TAMPA BAY A CHURCH
(MISSIONARY TO AMERICA)

In every generation the Lord has raised up people to lead the way to awakening. Jennifer LeClaire is one of those people in our generation. As an eyewitness to biblical transformation in Manchester, Kentucky (the City of Hope), I watched as the Lord brought us to desperation. Hope replaced despair, and the manifest presence of the Lord came into our city. We were changed forever. This book will stir you to pray and act upon the leading of the Holy Spirit. I pray this book reaches every Christian leader in America. Thank you, Jennifer, for your courage and insight. Awakening! Do it again, Lord! Our hope is in You.

—DOUG ABNER
DIRECTOR, APPALACHIAN CENTRE FOR TRANSFORMATION

Jennifer LeClaire has presented a compelling case for another great, national spiritual awakening in our land. Her passion for God, truth, and authentic revival shine through on every page. I highly recommend this book.

—EDDIE L. HYATT, DMIN
AUTHOR, *2000 YEARS OF CHARISMATIC CHRISTIANITY*

Jennifer LeClaire has done an amazing job bringing together the thoughts, vision, and insights of many key leaders who have a heart for revival! Her prophetic calling, gift of writing, and access to a vast array of pastors, prophetic leaders, and scholars have come forth in this delightful book that will not only inspire you but also inform you. Her passion for God and love for His people are clearly evident.

—JOSEPH MATTERA
PRESIDING BISHOP, CHRIST COVENANT COALITION
OVERSEEING BISHOP, RESURRECTION CHURCH

Revival is neither coincidental nor accidental. It is heaven's response to the intentional, fervent prayers of a people no longer satisfied with the status quo. In these last days the necessity for revival is evident. Even now God is ready to release a great outpouring of His spirit if His people will humbly position themselves in prayer and make an appeal to heaven. Jennifer LeClaire has skillfully brought together a chorus of voices from the revivalists of the past and present to pen a prophetic word for this hour. You're not holding this book by accident. There is already a stirring within you for more. What follows is a starting point for personal and national awakening.

—DANIEL K. NORRIS
EVANGELIST AND FORMER COHOST WITH THE LATE STEVE HILL,
FROM THE FRONT LINES

Jennifer LeClaire has done a masterful job of weaving together America's past history, its current condition, as well as God's future purposes. LeClaire has skillfully blended the many prophetic voices of the past and present, giving us a clear message of God's intended purpose for America. Revival!

This book is a call to arms for God's people to arise and join the ranks of those who will wrestle in prayer to see God's kingdom advanced in our nation.

—DAVID RAVENHILL
AUTHOR AND TEACHER

I really appreciate how Jennifer LeClaire ties us to the roots of awakening. America was born in awakening, and now God is returning us to our roots. Read this book, and let's arise to possess the land for Christ and His kingdom.

—KEN MALONE
FOUNDER, FORERUNNER MINISTRIES

The gifted pen of Jennifer LeClaire has proven to be a powerful tool to scribe the insight of many significant voices in *The Next Great Move of God*. The variety of voices provide a wonderfully unique and broad perspective for the singular hope of His coming. I encourage everyone to read this powerful book. It will encourage you to become a part of the story line of the next great move of God.

—RICK CURRY
FOUNDING APOSTLE, KING'S WAY CHURCH

This book is a must-read. It presents the cutting edge of what is and will become a very significant movement in this nation. Jennifer LeClaire's ability to focus on the truth and compile it in a matter that paints such a clear picture is a much-needed gift today. Her decision to use many other writers to contribute to this book is a very wise choice as it helps bring this message forth in a broad way. Thank you, Jennifer, for your contribution to the body of Christ!

—APOSTLE CLAY NASH
FOUNDER, THE CITYGATE

THE NEXT GREAT MOVE

of

GOD

JENNIFER LeCLAIRE

CHARISMA
HOUSE

Most Charisma House Book Group products are available at special quantity discounts for bulk purchase for sales promotions, premiums, fund-raising, and educational needs. For details, write Charisma House Book Group, 600 Rinehart Road, Lake Mary, Florida 32746, or telephone (407) 333-0600.

The Next Great Move of God by Jennifer LeClaire
Published by Charisma House
Charisma Media/Charisma House Book Group
600 Rinehart Road
Lake Mary, Florida 32746
www.charismahouse.com

Cover design by Justin Evans

Visit the author's website at www.JenniferLeClaire.org.

Library of Congress Cataloging-in-Publication Data:
LeClaire, Jennifer (Jennifer L.)
  The next great move of God / Jennifer LeClaire. -- First edition.
      pages cm
  Includes bibliographical references.
  ISBN 978-1-62998-616-6 (trade paper) -- ISBN 978-1-62998-617-3 (ebook)
  1. United States--Church history. 2. United States--Church history--21st century. 3. Christianity--United States--21st century. I. Title.
  BR515.L425 2015
  269--dc23
                                2014049633

First edition

15 16 17 18 19 — 987654321
Printed in the United States of America

This book is dedicated to the Pilgrims, Puritans, Pietists, pioneers, prophets, intercessors, and many others who have served God and the United States of America through the generations. I am grateful for the prayers they prayed, the gospel they preached, the miracles they worked, the prophecies they declared, and their hearts to see God's kingdom come and His will be done in America just as it is in heaven.

CONTENTS

ACKNOWLEDGMENTS

THERE ISN'T ROOM enough here for me to thank all those who helped make this book a reality as we moved quickly to chronicle a moment in time and an emerging move of God. The unity of the saints from many streams in the body of Christ made it possible.

I first want to thank Dutch Sheets for being willing to let me share the revelations that God shared with him, revelations that are impacting a nation.

I am also thankful to Rick Curry, Ken Malone, Clay Nash, Doug Abner, George Otis Jr., Reinhard Bonnke, Billy Graham, Doug Stringer, Cindy Jacobs, Rodney Howard-Browne, Jonathan Cahn, Eddie Hyatt, R. Loren Sandford, James Goll, David Ravenhill, Michael Brown, Mike Bickle, Daniel Norris, Larry Sparks, Joseph Mattera, and many others who contributed to this book.

I also want to thank Linda Willoughby and Michelle Smith for helping me pray it through. And thanks to Tessie DeVore and Debbie Marrie at Charisma House for seeing the vital need to chronicle what God is doing in the earth in this hour and to Adrienne Gaines for carefully working through the editing process.

FOREWORD

I HEARD THE Holy Spirit say, "I'm going to confirm to you tomorrow night through the passage of Scripture you read that I'm sending a Third Great Awakening to America."

The year was 1991, the place Washington, DC. It was the week of the National Day of Prayer, and I was about to participate in something they called a Biblethon. A canopy was set up on the Capitol grounds outfitted with a light, a podium, and a small PA system. Participants, in fifteen-minute increments, read through the entire Bible chronologically, declaring God's Word over Congress and our nation. No praying. No talking. Just declaring the Word of God. Obviously, readers weren't allowed to choose the passage they read—they simply continued reading from where the person ahead of them stopped. My slot was 2:00 a.m. that Wednesday.

When the Holy Spirit spoke to me of the confirmation He would give, my response was one of uncertainty. I knew I could find statements in almost any fifteen-minute Scripture reading from which I could concoct a revival connection. I could do so through a reference to His greatness, sovereignty, or mercy; or possibly from a passage in which He overthrew evil, performed a miracle, or promised salvation.

"Sorry, Lord," I said, "but I simply don't trust myself on this one. "Due to what I've been studying, writing about, and praying," I continued, "there is only one way I could be confident my Bible passage is confirmation of another great awakening coming to America: my passage would have to be either Haggai or Habakkuk."

I know this condition seems a little strange, but God had been speaking to me from those two books of the Bible for months. It did, however, seem impossible that this could occur. Just in case you're unaware of it, Haggai has two chapters and Habakkuk has three! What are the odds that when my timeslot arrived the progression of the reading would be precisely at one of those books? Minuscule.

"Again Lord, if this is You speaking to me, I'm sorry," I continued, "but this is the only way I could believe I wasn't simply 'conjuring up' a confirmation."

I arrived thirty minutes early, signed the roster, and enjoyed listening to others read. No surprise—they were nowhere near Haggai or Habakkuk. "Oh well, no confirmation tonight," I thought, "but I'll still enjoy reading and decreeing God's Word over our government and nation."

A couple minutes before my time arrived, the person in charge approached me with the standard alert: "You're on deck, Mr. Sheets."

"Yes, ma'am."

Then she paused and with a somewhat confused expression said, "And when you read, you have your choice. You can either read the Book of Haggai or the Book of Habakkuk."

I was stunned! "Excuse me?" I mumbled.

With the same disoriented and puzzled look, she repeated the choice. "Haggai or Habakkuk." I'm still not sure she even knew why she was doing this.

"I'll read Habakkuk," I muttered, in a shocked state of mind. And then, probably with more faith than I ever had in my entire life, I read and decreed God's Word over our nation. And when I came to chapter 2 of Habakkuk, I almost screamed the words of the first three verses:

> I will stand on my guard post and station myself on the rampart; and I will keep watch to see what He will speak to me, and how I may reply when I am reproved. Then the LORD answered me and said, "Record the vision and inscribe it on tablets, that the one who reads it may run. For the vision is yet for the appointed time; it hastens toward the goal and it will not fail. Though it tarries, wait for it; for it will certainly come, it will not delay."
>
> —NAS

I have been praying for revival in America since the 1980s after the height of the Jesus People and charismatic movements. I burn with passion to see our nation visited again with a mighty outpouring of the Holy Spirit. And though the vision has indeed tarried, I, like Abraham and Sarah who waited twenty-five years for Isaac, am confident that He who promised is faithful. I am confident as well that America's Redeemer lives and that His mercy will triumph over judgment.

A Third Great Awakening is coming to America!

Many spiritual leaders also have come to believe this. You'll read about them in this book. Hope will rise and your faith will be stirred as you read what the Holy Spirit is saying to them. And I hope you'll be stirred to pray.

When you see that our nation was born under an amazing flag emblazoned with the words "Appeal to Heaven," perhaps you will be inspired to make your appeal. This banner, with its blatant dependence on God, flew over our naval vessels, government buildings, and battlefields. The colonists knew it was ludicrous to think they could defeat Great Britain…unless heaven intervened. If the United States of America was God's will—not just the dream of some folks seeking liberty—and He wanted to birth a new nation by giving them success, then they could prevail. "Let's appeal to heaven!" was their plan for victory.

As Jennifer LeClaire chronicles in this book, God is bringing this flag back to the forefront in America. Why? Because He is trying to reconnect us to our godly roots and to the fact that America was His idea. He needed a nation such as ours that would partner with Him around the world. Today the Lord wants us to put His dream back into "the American dream," so that He can heal our land, send us a Third Great Awakening, and restore our destiny.

Jennifer makes this clear and makes the case that the time for this is now. Read this book! Allow your heart to dream with God about a nation reborn, about partnering with Him to birth and spread the greatest awakening America and the world have ever experienced.

You were born for such a time as this—seize the day!

—DUTCH SHEETS
INTERNATIONAL PRAYER LEADER AND CONFERENCE SPEAKER
AUTHOR, *APPEAL TO HEAVEN*

Introduction

IT'S TIME TO WAKE UP

Wнen Messianic rabbi Jonathan Cahn's book *The Harbinger* hit the *New York Times* best-seller list the week it released in print, I believe the sleeping giant called the church started waking up.

A prophetic warning to the American masses about God's impending judgment on the nation, *The Harbinger* connects undeniable dots between what has happened in the United States since the terrorist attacks in 2001—including a housing market bust and banking industry collapse that led to a $700 billion government bailout to prop up financial institutions and auto manufacturers—and Israel's fate after it turned away from Jehovah God. Although written as a fictional narrative, the book details how nine signs hidden in recent events reveal God's progressive judgment on America.

Here's the message in a nutshell: Cahn believes the Holy Spirit showed him that events such as 9/11, the collapse of Wall Street, and the Great Recession occurred because God lifted some of His hedge of protection from around America. He is certain God is trying to get our attention. He is convinced that God is warning the nation to turn back to Him and used nine harbingers, or prophetic signs, to shake us up and wake us up. *The Harbinger* may anger some; it may scare others. It caused some to fall to their knees in repentance, and it caused others to cry out in intercession.

The release of *The Harbinger* was what you could call a "*kairos* moment"—a supreme moment in time when God sent a prophet with a "you need to hear this and repent" message to America. Notice I say "to America"—not just to the church in America. Cahn's message about an ancient mystery that holds the secret to America's future transcended the Christian market to become a mainstream phenomenon that, at the time of this writing, is still on the *New York Times* best-seller list nearly three years later.

The book—and the clear proof of God's discipline on our nation—changed my theology. Until 2012 I did not believe God sent judgments on nations in the New Testament age. I reasoned that if God were going to judge any nation, He would start with places like the Netherlands, with cities like Amsterdam and its infamous Red Light District that hosts all manner of immorality. But the founders of the Netherlands didn't make and break a covenant with God.

I believe America as a nation is reaping what we've sown. I believe that where there is unfettered sin, there is ultimately death (Rom. 6:23). And although some rightly argue that many nations are more sinful and anti-God than the United States, consider this: to whom much is given, much is required (Luke 12:48). As a world power, the United States has done much good. But our nation's Christian foundations are shaking. The seven major influencers of our society—the economy, government, family, spirituality, education, media, and arts—are shaping an idolatrous New Age culture.

I submit to you that our nation is in natural and spiritual crisis, and it will take a divine intervention to avert disaster. Although "man" can't solve the problems in our nation, electing leaders who will guide the United States using biblical principles rather than those who defy biblical principles in the name of change speaks volumes to heaven. Politicians can't fix what's broken, but politicians who pray to the One who can will receive His wisdom to right the ship.

If we don't make a drastic shift in this nation, I believe there's no way to escape God's judgment. Billy Graham's late wife, Ruth, once said, "If God doesn't judge America He will have to apologize to Sodom and Gomorrah."[1] Again, I never wanted to believe that. But now I do. I can see it. God has removed some of our hedge of protection because He loves us and hopes we'll wake up. We haven't woken up yet—but clearly there is an awakening afoot.

A Third Great Awakening

On April 21, 2007, the Lord woke me up at midnight with a prophetic word that I didn't fully understand. Mind you, this was before the housing bubble burst, before the banks and financial institutions started to fail, before the US government bailout, before President Obama was elected, before the Great Recession that rippled through the world and eventually saw economies completely fail, before the Ebola scare, and before ISIS emerged as a credible threat on American soil. Before we—or at least before I—understood our desperate need for a great awakening, the Holy Spirit spoke these words to me:

> There is a great awakening coming to this nation, for I have heard your cries and I long to heal your land. I am a covenant God, and I will not forget the

covenant I made with your founding forefathers. Yes, there will be a shaking, but the foundations will not crack and they will not crumble. Only those things which can be shaken will be shaken that the sin in the land may be laid bare.

Repentance. I require repentance from My people who have through the generations allowed the enemy to take ground in this nation. I require repentance for the abortions and for the prayerlessness. I require repentance for the apathy and for the idolatry. You shall have no other gods before me. I am indeed the God of America.

Yes, there is a great awakening coming to this nation. I am the author of it, and I will bring it to pass. Just turn from your wicked ways and humble yourselves. Stand in the gap and make up the hedge. I am the Lord, and I am a warrior. I will not leave or forsake this country. I will fight through you and with you to regain what has been lost.

Be encouraged now, because as you go forth boldly with My Word and My Spirit, there will be the sound of truth, and it will prevail in the land. Speak boldly and clearly, and watch as the mighty men arise to take their positions on the wall and in the churches and in the marketplaces, for I am raising up deliverers and reformers in this generation who will not shrink back at the challenge that is coming in the days ahead.

Yes, it will grow darker before My light shines brightly from this nation again. But the light has not been extinguished and will not be extinguished. The time to rise up is now. I am calling you to war. I am calling you to repentance. I am calling you to My side. I am the captain of the hosts. I am calling you to victory. I am calling you to destiny. Will you answer?

There is hope for America. I believe the remnant is rising. But it has certainly gotten darker in this nation, and again, I fear God's judgment may fall harder if we continue to stand by in silence while abortion, same-sex marriage, and other sin rages in our land.

The church—the "sleeping giant"—needs to wake up. If the church were being the church, we wouldn't have so many problems in our nation. Of course, these problems didn't start just four years ago. There has been an increasingly rapid decline in morality in this nation since prayer was removed from schools in 1962. Abortion was legalized in 1973. Massachusetts became the first state to legalize gay marriage in 2004. And plenty of wickedness has taken place in between and since.

What if we all lived the Sermon on the Mount lifestyle? The Sermon on the Mount lifestyle makes no room for even the thought of murder, which is what abortion really is. The Sermon on the Mount lifestyle shuns sexual immorality, which includes homosexuality. The Sermon on the Mount lifestyle would radically change our hearts—and, I believe, the heart of a nation. But much of the church is largely ignoring the Sermon on the Mount's Christianity 101 lessons. The church looks, thinks, and acts too much like the world. Christians are having abortions. Christians are committing adultery. Christians are fornicating. Christians are getting divorced. Lord, help us!

At the same time, the Sermon on the Mount speaks to giving to the needy, prayer, and fasting. I can't prove it with hard numbers, but it's likely that most Christians aren't giving to the poor. It's probable that most Christians aren't praying for our nation. And I'm quite sure most Christians aren't fasting. We really aren't serving as salt and light. And that's ultimately why our society is becoming more tasteless and continues to grow darker.

Adding insult to this injurious lifestyle, some Christians declare that prayer rallies and solemn assemblies don't make a difference. I believe the greatest sin of the church is prayerlessness. The government of the world is in the prayer rooms. Yet many are too busy feeding their souls on worldly entertainment to meet God at the altar. Many others don't have faith to pray in the midst of the pressures, stress, and strain of life.

There Is Hope

The shaking is undeniable. Natural disasters are claiming lives in America. Economic disasters are driving poverty in America. Agronomists are predicting famine in America. Politicians are being shot in America. Protesters are taking to the streets in America. All the while some Americans are armed for another civil war.

Our nation is in crisis. It has grown darker since the Lord spoke that prophetic word to me in 2007. It will continue growing darker until we turn back to God as a nation. The good news is that when we do, we'll see a great awakening, and many souls will come into the kingdom. There will be a great harvest. I'm blowing the trumpet. I'm sounding the alarm. There is hope for America, and that hope lies in the body of Christ rising up to do as Jesus commanded: "Occupy till I come" (Luke 19:13, KJV). Of course, we have to wake up first.

It would be easy to dismiss Cahn's revelation about America's future, which is based on a pattern found in Isaiah 9:10 after God temporarily lifted the hedge of protection around Israel and an enemy struck the land. Yet the message of *The Harbinger* has resonated with millions of Americans—and even found its way into the hands of government officials. In 2012 Cahn's publisher, Charisma House, sent a copy of the book to every member of Congress so they could hear what God is saying to the nation.

We live in sobering times. I believe we're living in the last days when, like the apostle Paul said, "Men will be lovers of themselves, lovers of money, boastful, proud, blasphemers, disobedient to parents, unthankful, unholy, without natural affection, trucebreakers, slanderers, unrestrained, fierce, despisers of those who are good, traitors, reckless, conceited, lovers of pleasures more than lovers of God, having a form of godliness, but denying its power" (2 Tim. 3:2–5).

I believe we're living at the end of the age when, as Jesus said:

> Many will come in My name, saying, "I am the Christ," and will deceive many. You will hear of wars and rumors of wars. See that you are not troubled. For all these things must happen, but the end is not yet. For nation will rise against nation, and kingdom against kingdom. There will be famines, epidemics, and earthquakes in various places. All these are the beginning of sorrows.
>
> Then they will hand you over to be persecuted and will kill you. And you will be hated by all nations for My name's sake. Then many will fall away, and betray one another, and hate one another. And many false prophets will rise and will deceive many. Because iniquity will abound, the love of many will grow cold. But he who endures to the end shall be saved. And this gospel of the kingdom will be preached

throughout the world as a testimony to all nations, and then the end will come.

—MATTHEW 24:5–14

I believe time is short for America to repent before we see stronger manifestations of God's discipline on this nation, but at the same time I have never been more hopeful. I believe that we are on a cusp of a Third Great Awakening even now. And I believe the Lord is using *The Harbinger* to sound an alarm that will wake up the mighty men and women, the reformers and deliverers who will stand in the gap and make up the hedge. But God is not just using *The Harbinger*. He's also using prophetic voices such as Dutch Sheets with his "Appeal to Heaven" message, Billy Graham with his "My Hope" initiative, Reinhard Bonnke with his trumpet call that "All America shall be saved," and many others.

So let this book wake you up to the realities our nation is facing, but let it also fill you with hope, and let that hope give substance to your faith to pray and take action as you agree with God's plan for America to wake up in this hour.

Chapter 1

THE SPIRITUAL STATE
OF THE UNION

EVERY YEAR THE president of the United States offers a State of the Union address that presents to Congress the administration's view of the nation's condition. Whether the president is Republican or Democrat, that speech is always bullish about our national prospects for education, manufacturing, farming, employment, the housing market, federal debt reduction, and so on.

In his 2014 State of the Union address President Obama declared the results of his administration's efforts, explaining that America now has:

> The lowest unemployment rate in over five years. A rebounding housing market. A manufacturing sector that's adding jobs for the first time since the 1990s. More oil produced at home than we buy from the rest of the world—the first time that's happened in nearly twenty years. Our deficits—cut by more than half. And for the first time in over a decade, business leaders around the world have declared that China is no longer the world's number one place to invest; America is.[1]

He went to declare: "That's why I believe this can be a breakthrough year for America. After five years of grit and determined effort, the United States is better-positioned for the twenty-first century than any other nation on earth."[2] And he ended his speech with these words: "Believe it. God bless you, and God bless the United States of America."[3]

Although it's true that statistics in key areas such as employment, housing starts, and manufacturing show some improvement over five years ago, this is no real reason to rejoice at the state of our union from a spiritual perspective. Indeed, these statistics are merely whitewash that's making a land full of corruption on the inside look bright and shiny on the outside—or at least brighter and shinier than it really is. In order to understand the true state of the union, one has to look at the fruit and drill down to the roots of belief systems infecting American culture.

Severing Our Lifeline to God

I believe the rapid decline of American society began on June 25, 1962, when the church allowed prayer to be removed from public schools. In 1962 the US Supreme Court examined a twenty-two-word prayer children used to acknowledge God. That prayer went like this: "Almighty God, we acknowledge our dependence upon Thee, and we beg Thy blessings upon us, our parents, our teachers, and our Country."[4] It's a simple but powerful prayer that I believe invoked God's protection over schools and inspired morality in the hearts of a generation. Removing prayer from public schools has spawned a well-documented impact on our educational system and on the broader society.

In his book *America: To Pray or Not to Pray* David Barton offers statistics on the impact of removing prayer from schools. I won't recount all the numbers here. Suffice it to say that there has been a dramatic rise in premarital sex, sexually transmitted diseases, teenage pregnancy, unmarried mothers, single-parent households, unwed couples living together, the divorce rate, alcohol consumption per capita, violent crime, illegal drug use, and abortions. Across the board the nation has witnessed a dramatic rise in immorality, and it grew at a precipitous pace when prayer was removed from schools. Prayer is our lifeline to God, and once that lifeline is severed, we begin to see manifestations of death.

"Prayer, an acknowledgement of God, is the simplest identification of a philosophy which recognizes not only the God of heaven but also His laws and standards of conduct," wrote Barton, founder of WallBuilders, an organization dedicated to presenting American's forgotten history and heroes, with an emphasis on moral, religious, and constitutional foundation on which America was built. "Prayer, being the 'heart' of religion, was by necessity the first target of a general attack on all religious principles...After the removal of prayer, there quickly followed cases rejecting not only the Bible but also any values derived from them—the Ten Commandments, the teaching of pre-marital sexual abstinence to students, etc."[5]

Skeptics will deny any correlation between prayer in schools and morality in our nation, but I beg to differ—and the numbers don't lie. By giving children the opportunity to participate in a corporate prayer every morning from the time they were old enough to attend school, America's youth were exposed to the person and power of God. By shutting God out of the school system, many children lost the chance to invite Him into their families and into their hearts. The Word of God says to "pray without ceasing" (1 Thess. 5:17), to "pray in the Spirit always with all kinds of prayer and supplication" (Eph. 6:18), to "continue in prayer, and be watchful with thanksgiving" (Col. 4:2), and "that the men should pray everywhere" (1 Tim. 2:8). Stealing the destiny of a generation—and, in fact, generations, started with the attack on school prayer.

Barton notes:

> The removal of prayer was the first step on the infamous "slippery slope." While the removal of school prayer cannot be blamed for all the declines, the presence or absence, legality or illegality, of prayer and the acknowledgment of God in public arenas is the primary indicator of the philosophy under which official public policy is being conducted. When there is an official recognition of prayer—"the quintessential religious practice"—there is also an embracing of the values and teachings of which prayer is a primary indicator.[6]

Clearly our nation needs God now more than ever. Allowing students to participate in a moment of prayer every morning is not a panacea for our nation's problems, but it is one step in the right direction as atheists, humanists, secularists, and other anti-Christ champions continue working to remove God from our public square.

The good news is a remnant is awakening even in the schools. Young women like Oneida High School cheerleader Asia Canada prays at the beginning of a football game despite the school's ban on prayer.[7] And men like Tom Brittain, head varsity coach at Tempe Preparatory Academy in Arizona, are praying with their teams afterward.[8] Shows like *Duck Dynasty* are inspiring school prayer clubs, and states like Mississippi and North Carolina are making strong moves to get Christian prayer back in schools.[9]

There's an awakening afoot, and we need to join with these courageous ones in prayer for, yes, the right to pray in public. I believe God has been waiting for His people to rise up with a unified voice of righteousness against the immorality in this nation. I believe God has been patient through our prayerlessness. And I believe if we set our hearts toward reinstituting Christian prayer in schools, it could fuel the prophesied great awakening in this generation.

The Fruit of Prayerlessness

Barton offered an overview of the rapid decline of immorality and crime since prayer was removed from schools. However, in examining the spiritual state of our union, it's worth drilling down into some more shocking manifestations of the slippery slope the church is sliding down even now.

According to the Guttmacher Institute, about 1.21 million abortions were performed in the United States in 2008—and based on that rate, one-third of American women will have had at least one abortion by the age of forty-five.[10] Thirty-seven percent of women obtaining abortions identify themselves as Protestant, and 28 percent as Catholic.[11] This all began in 1973 with *Roe v. Wade* when the church allowed a law to pass that legalized abortion. Psalm 139:13–14 makes clear the sanctity of life: "You brought my inner parts into being; You wove me in my mother's womb. I will praise you, for You made me with fear and wonder; marvelous are Your works, and You know me completely."

As of December 2014 gay marriage was legal in thirty-five states.[12] The attack on God-ordained marriage is raging. This is despite the fact that Hebrews 13:4 says, "Marriage is to be honored among everyone, and the bed undefiled. But God will judge the sexually immoral and adulterers," and 1 Corinthians 6:9–10 clearly states that, "Neither the sexually immoral, nor idolaters, nor adulterers, nor male prostitutes, nor homosexuals, nor thieves, nor covetous, nor drunkards, nor revilers, nor extortioners will inherit the kingdom of God."

In light of these and other scriptures, it's especially disturbing that Christian denominations are embracing gay marriage. The United Church of Christ, which considers itself a mainline Protestant denomination—claiming over one million members and about fifty-two hundred congregations in the United States—proudly sponsored the 2014 Gay Games as part of its "progressive Christianity."[13]

In case you aren't familiar with what the term "progressive Christianity" really means, let's take a moment to define it. Progressive Christianity has a strong focus on social justice and environmentalism. Progressive Christianity focuses on concepts such as "collective salvation"—where entire cultures and societies, rather than just individuals with faith in Christ, are redeemed—and bends toward a Marxist economic philosophy. Progressive Christianity also does not subscribe to the biblical doctrine of the inerrancy of Scripture.

But even denominations that don't consider themselves part of the Progressive Christianity movement are falling into this deception. The Presbyterian Church (USA) in 2014 voted to allow its ministers to perform gay weddings in states where it's legal.[14] Also in 2014, Methodist Pastor Frank

Schaefer, who was defrocked for officiating his son's same-sex wedding, was fully reinstated.[15] And the Moravians voted to ordain gay clergy.[16] My research shows there's a long and growing list of gay-affirming denominations.

The good news is many denominations are standing against the rising gay rights tide. The Assemblies of God, among other Pentecostal denominations, firmly supports traditional marriage. And the Southern Baptist Convention's Executive Committee recently voted to break ties with a California church when it was discovered that leadership was affirming homosexual behavior.[17]

It speaks volumes that Christian leaders speaking out against gay marriage are receiving death threats even as the mainstream media push TV shows that portray gay, lesbian, bisexual, and transgendered people, as well as polygamists and practitioners of polyamory. Some want to see pedophilia emerge as the next civil rights issue.[18] And some Christian pastors are bringing New Age philosophies into the pulpit. Many are declaring peace where there is no peace while the enemy keeps rocking a sleeping church and whitewashing the situation. (See Jeremiah 6:14; Ezekiel 13:10.)

The Spiritual Avalanche

In December 2012 the late evangelist Steve Hill, perhaps best known for his preaching in the Brownsville Revival that saw millions experience an outpouring in Pensacola, Florida, in the 1990s, warned of the rise of false teaching. He later penned a book called *Spiritual Avalanche: The Threat of False Teachings That Could Destroy Millions*. This was the last book published before he died and offers some incredible revelation to the body of Christ. I'll share the basics of his vision here, but it's worth picking up the book to get the whole picture:

> A few days ago, after enjoying quality time with Jesus, I was surprised by an alarming vision. I saw a massive, majestic mountain covered in glistening snow. It reminded me of the Matterhorn in the Swiss Alps. Its peaks were sparkling white, and I was amazed by God's attention to detail. It was so realistic I wanted to go skiing! But I sensed there was more that the Holy Spirit was about to reveal.
>
> As I closed my eyes, the entire mountainside sparkled with lights. I was in a winter wonderland bustling with thousands of vacationers. The ski lodge, condos, hotels, and cabins were at full capacity at this popular resort. The visiting five-star rich, the indebted middle class, and the locals who scrubbed the floors were all part of this picturesque parade...
>
> I began to discern the details. The excited skiers were not anticipating any danger. And why should they be? They had invested hard-earned money to be at a safe, highly recommended, popular family resort.
>
> The Christian faith is almost identical. Innocent lambs have joined churches, paid their tithes, volunteered, and fellowshipped—all based on a naive trust that the leadership is everything it purports to be. They love the entertainment and enjoy the spoon-fed meals. Meanwhile snow continues to cover the mountain.
>
> I was amazed to be seeing such detail in this vision. But why not? Our God is the master of the meticulous. He paints butterflies, creates billions of unique human beings, makes sure that no two snowflakes are alike, and continually controls the circle of life.

Day quickly turned to night. The skiers, snow-boarders, and sports enthusiasts were settling in. Anticipation grew as the snow began to fall. It seemed that everyone headed to bed believing tomorrow would be a day of sheer enjoyment on freshly covered slopes. For an avid skier the exhilaration of being the first one to race down a new blanket of snow is a dream come true.

Throughout the night winter storms dropped several feet of new snow on the slopes. The night ski patrol was put on full alert. Their mission was clear. With the potential of killer avalanches occurring, they quickly took to their posts. Most readers are familiar with the word *avalanche*. By definition it is "a sudden overwhelming appearance and deluge of snow, ice, and mud." It comes from a French word that means "to fall or let down."

I began to weep as the vision, along with its spiritual application, continued to unfold.

The ski patrol operated like a well-trained platoon. Some boarded helicopters manned with small bombs; others jumped on snowmobiles loaded with handheld explosive devices. What seemed to be a strategic group of sharpshooters were stationed at the base, maneuvering anti-tank weapons aimed at the snow-covered peaks. They fired their weapons at strategic points in the avalanche zone to force avalanches before the snow accumulated to a life-threatening depth. Left unchecked, the accumulation of heavy, dense snow packed on top of lighter snow could easily slide down with incredible speed and force, resulting in enormous damage and loss of life.

The Lord began to speak. I trembled.

The fresh, new snow represents false teaching that

is steadily falling on the ears of the body of Christ. It has been, and is, a heavy snowfall. The skiers represent believers and nonbelievers trusting the resort for a safe and memorable experience. As Christians we have been warned in Scripture: "Be sober, be vigilant; because your adversary the devil walks about like a roaring lion, seeking whom he may devour" (1 Pet. 5:8, NKJV). However, several currently popular, awe-inspiring teachings have lulled many into a deep sleep.

Layers upon layers of snow have been steadily covering the solid, traditional truth of Christ. God's Word tells us that foolish teaching in these days will become so fashionable even the most dedicated believer can become deceived. "For false christs and false prophets will rise and show great signs and wonders to deceive, if possible, even the elect" (Matt. 24:24, NKJV). It's happening before our eyes. One spiritual leader said the other day, "You guys are old-fashioned 'holiness.' We are modern-day 'grace.' You live in bondage, while we can do anything we want."

Pastors and teachers worldwide have succumbed to heretical teachings, including universal reconciliation, deification of man, challenging the validity of the Word of God including His judgments, and even lifting any boundaries, claiming His amazing grace is actually "amazing freedom." You are free to live according to your own desires. Sound familiar? "In those days there was no king in Israel; everyone did what was right in his own eyes" (Judg. 17:6, NKJV). Many popular, self-proclaimed ministers of the gospel are covering the slopes and will be held accountable for the spiritual death of millions.

Just as the ski patrol did in this vision, those who

are aware of what's happening must take swift and accurate action. Their weapons of warfare must be aimed at the peaks and the avalanche terrain to dispel the lies. Apostles, prophets, evangelists, pastors, and teachers must be willing to drop spiritual bombs, fire anti-heresy missiles, and even drive into the danger zones armed with explosive truth to confront this potential avalanche. The spiritual generals of this generation must leave the war room and put their years of experience on the front lines.

Friend, I humbly encourage you to heed this vision and take it before the Lord. This is not just Steve Hill telling a story. I've written it just as it was given, and I've expounded the details in this book under the direction of the Holy Spirit. My responsibility is to share with the body of Christ His words to me. The ears that hear and the hands that obey are out of my control.

Satan is "snowing" the saints, but it can be stopped. In the vision I heard explosions. I saw dedicated Christian soldiers scrambling to do anything it took to bring down this avalanche before devastation occurred.

One of the most powerful weapons we possess to combat this onslaught is the tongue. Let God set yours ablaze by preaching "all the words in red." ...If we take action *now*, the result will be a tearing down of false teaching and a remaining layer of solid, God-given, biblical instruction that will save the lost, heal the sick, and strengthen Christians to do the true work of the ministry.[19]

Religion Losing Its Influence?

According to the Pew Research Center, 72 percent of the public now thinks religion is losing influence in American life. That's up five percentage points from 2010 to the highest level in Pew Research polling over the past decade.[20] The silver lining is that most people who say religion's influence is waning actually see this as a bad thing.

There is room for the church to rise up and be salt and light again—and we need to act swiftly because American sentiment about the union itself is growing bitter. A September 2014 Reuters poll asked: "Do you support or oppose the idea of your state peacefully withdrawing from the United States of America and the federal government?" Nearly 24 percent said they were "strongly or provisionally inclined" to leave the United States.[21] A remnant of believers is awakening and speaking out.

"America is a nation at war. This is not a war being fought with guns and bombs; it's being fought with words and ideas," says Mike Huckabee, former Arkansas governor, former Republican presidential nominee, and the host of Fox News' *Huckabee*. "We aren't sending armies to face off with our enemy, but there are definitely opposing sides in a confrontation."[22]

Huckabee goes on to explain that the battle isn't taking place on foreign soil; it's right on our doorstep—and the casualties are mounting daily. Of course, he's talking about a culture war, what he calls a battle for the religious freedom of our forefathers embedded into the very first amendment of our nation's bill of rights.

"We're living at a crucial point in history. Many around us are sleeping. They aren't aware of the plan that is already underway to steal our freedoms right out from underneath us," Huckabee continues. "...If our generation stays asleep or chooses to stand by and do nothing in this battle, the America our children and grandchildren inherit from us will be completely unrecognizable to us, let alone our country's Founding Fathers."[23]

We need another great awakening.

When it comes to the culture wars, President Obama calls those standing for righteousness bitter. Todd Starnes, a Fox News reporter, prefers to be called blessed. As he sees it, the only reason we're clinging to our guns, our Bibles, and our jugs of sweet tea is because we're afraid the government is going to take them away from us.

"What the nation needs is a prophetic voice. But even our churches have been corrupted by the culture—turned into trendy nightclubs where good looks trump good character. Some preachers have traded the Word of God for pithy, self-help gimmickry," Starnes writes. "And in those rare instances when some pastors have taken to their bully pulpits to rail against anti-Christian bigotry, their outrage rings hollow. They issue utterances of condemnation, telling us it's once again time to draw a line in the sand. Unfortunately, it's too late. We're already knee-deep in the ocean."[24]

We need another great awakening.

Prophetic Voices Rising

Thank God, prophetic voices are arising who are bold enough to speak the truth. The late D. James Kennedy, the former pastor of Coral Ridge Presbyterian Church who produced a weekly television and radio show called *Truths That Transform*, launched gospel missiles in the culture war long before it was popular. Before he went home to be with the Lord in 2007, he said things like this:

> Today, secular humanism has virtually become the established religion of this country in the public schools of America. "There is no God." "People were not created. They simply evolved from the primeval slime by some chance concatenation of amino acids." "There are no moral absolutes. We cannot, therefore, call upon anyone to do anything. Whose morality shall we impose?"
>
> You see, after getting rid of prayer and the Bible in the schools, it was inevitable that the Supreme Court would rule that the Ten Commandments could not be posted on the walls of the schools in Kentucky. Religion, morality—legislation. Now we are rudderless. Whose morality, indeed? We must get back to our roots. You cannot run a nation without morality. Without some transcendent morality, it is simply the stronger imposing the will upon the other. If there is no God to support a morality, why should anyone follow it? Why is your morality better than his, or her morality better than yours?
>
> This is where America has come because we have been cut loose from our moorings. We do not know where we are going because we do not know from whence we have come.[25]

Dr. Ben Carson, a retired neurosurgeon and best-selling author of *One Nation: What We Can All Do to Save America*, sent shockwaves through the media and inspired the remnant with his February 2013 speech at the National Prayer Breakfast. He started by reading four scriptures from the Word of God: Proverbs 11:9, Proverbs

11:12, Proverbs 11:25, and 2 Chronicles 7:14. Although he made it clear he wasn't trying to offend anyone, least of all President Obama who was sitting just a few feet away, he didn't hold back about the condition of our nation. And he hasn't slowed down since.

Carson wrote in his book *One Nation*:

> A quick glance at a newspaper should be enough to perceive the warning signs. As far as education is concerned, we have made a lot of progress in being politically correct, but very little progress in basic education, particularly in areas like math and science. The secular progressive movement completely denies any moral backsliding and feels that we have made substantial progress as a nation with respect to great moral issues like abortion, gay marriage, and helping the poor, but in reality we are losing our moral compass and are caught up in elitism and bigotry. On top of that, our national debt and the passage of Obamacare are threatening the financial future of our nation. Worst of all, we seem to have lost our ability to discuss important issues respectfully and courteously and cannot come together enough to begin to solve our problems.[26]

We need another great awakening.

Jonathan Cahn, a Messianic Jewish rabbi and pastor best known for his best-selling book *The Harbinger*, is one prophetic voice who has the ear of our government, even though some may not like what he says. At the Presidential Inaugural Prayer Breakfast in 2013 Cahn brought a message that he admitted from the onset may not be "politically correct" but was absolutely biblical. In his keynote address he compared ancient Israel with modern-day America:

In ancient times, there was a nation known as the kingdom of Israel. It had been founded on God's word, dedicated to His will, and consecrated to His purposes. And God blessed it with prosperity, power, security, peace, and a place at the head of nations. But the people of Israel made a fatal mistake; in the midst of their blessings, they turned away from God. They began to remove Him from their lives. Step by step they ruled Him out of their culture, out of their government, out of their economy, out of their public square, out of the instruction and lives of their children; they ruled Him out of the kingdom. They would still at times invoke His name, but it was increasingly hollow and meaningless. They had made themselves strangers to the God of their fathers and their foundation.

And as God was driven from their lives, they brought in foreign gods and idols to replace Him, gods of sensuality, materialism, violence; idols of wealth, carnality, and sexual promiscuity. They abandoned the ways of God, the laws of God, the standards of God for immorality. As the prophets cried out, they now called evil, "good," and good, "evil." What they once knew to be immoral, they now celebrated, and what they once knew to be right, they now warred against. It was a culture turned in upon itself, a civilization at war against the very foundation on which it had been established. And the righteous, who simply remained true to what they had once all known to be true, were now vilified, marginalized, mocked, labeled "intolerant," increasingly banned from the public square, and, ultimately, persecuted. The nation's culture grew increasingly vulgar, godless, and darkened. They now defiled, ridiculed, and blasphemed the name of God. It was as if a spiritual amnesia had overtaken the kingdom, as if they had never known God or His ways. And they descended into the darkest sins of the nations which surrounded them. They offered up their children as sacrifices to the gods, on the altars and fires of Baal and Molech. And they now stood under the shadow of judgment and in danger of destruction.

And God called out to them, to return, to come back, to be saved from destruction. He sent to them seers and prophets to wake them up, to call them back. But they wouldn't listen. They mocked the prophets and persecuted them. And they hardened their hearts. And finally something happened that brought them into the first stage of judgment.[27]

Does this sound like America to you? Cahn went on to connect the dots and paint a clear picture of an America that looks spiritually much like the nation of Israel in ancient days. America was founded in covenant with God, and God has blessed the nation mightily, but we have slowly, surely, and largely turned away from Him. Even our own president is declaring that America is no longer a Christian nation. If a Martian came to the earth and tried to match biblical Christianity to American Christianity, he would have to conclude Obama is right.

"The city on the hill has grown dark. Its lamp has grown dim. Its glory is fading. For God is not mocked. No nation can war against the very source of its blessings and expect those blessings to remain. And as it was with ancient Israel, the city on the hill now stands under the shadow of judgment," Cahn said. "...The time is late. The hour is critical. A great nation proceeds in rapid spiritual descent. And the signs of warning and judgment are manifesting in the land. The shadow of judgment is upon us."[28]

Cindy Jacobs, cofounder of Generals International, put it this way: "America is desperately in need of another great awakening. As many other nations in history have belatedly discovered, one cannot eliminate the name of Jesus and think that God does not see."[29] Evangelist Rodney Howard-Browne, pastor at The River at Tampa Bay, is even more direct: "Without divine intervention, what we call America will be gone within the next couple of years. It's that critical. The handwriting is on the wall. Only God can save us now. This is not a game. If we don't see a turn in the next two or three years, America as we know it will sink into the abyss and will be gone forever."[30]

Can you see that God is sending prophetic voices to warn America—even our very government and president? And yet little has changed. Our national debt continues piling up, abortions are still legal, prayerlessness abounds, a spiritual avalanche is threatening our churches even as dangers such as the Ebola virus and the Islamic state threaten to cross our borders. No politician can fix the problems our nation is facing. We need another great awakening. We need to make an appeal to heaven. The good news is that God wants to bring another spiritual awakening to America. He's just waiting for us to get in line with His Spirit.

Chapter 2

OUR EVERLASTING
COVENANT GOD

WHEN HAMAN THREATENED to murder the Israelites, Queen Esther made an appeal to Persia's King Ahasuerus to show mercy and bring justice (Esther 8). When the Jews falsely accused the apostle Paul with charges they could not prove, he appealed to Caesar, the Roman leader, for justice (Acts 25:11). Throughout the Psalms David appealed to the King of the universe for mercy and justice. Across Matthew, Mark, Luke, and John, Jews and Gentiles alike appealed to King Jesus for healing and deliverance—and miracles.

Making an appeal to the king is a principle that plays out repeatedly in Scripture from both a natural and spiritual perspective. One Shunammite woman picked up on this principle by listening to a prophet pray.

Here's the backstory: This Shunammite's husband was old, and they had no children. Elisha prophesied that this woman—the one who kept a warm bed and a hot plate waiting for him when he traveled through town—would have a baby boy to call her own the following year. His prophecy was spot-on. A baby was born, but the enemy waited for a strategic moment to try to kill the promise of God. The boy hit his head and died. When Elisha heard about it, he returned to Shunem to make an appeal to the King.

> When Elisha came into the house, he saw that the boy was dead, lying on his bed. So he went in, and shut the door on the two of them, and *prayed to the LORD*. He went up and lay on the child, put his face on his face, and his eyes on his eyes, and his hands on his hands. Then he bent over the child, and the child's flesh warmed. Then he got down, walked once back and forth in the house, and went up, and bent over him; the boy sneezed seven times, and the boy opened his eyes.
>
> —2 KINGS 4:32–35, EMPHASIS ADDED

In prophesying the birth of her child and then raising him from the dead by the power of God, Elisha more than won the confidence of the Shunammite woman. So when he came to her with a warning about a devastating famine that was about to hit the land of Israel, her ears perked up. Of course, true prophets do more than prophesy the warning—they also prophesy the way of escape when there is one. That's just what Elisha did. Elisha warned the Shunammite woman, but he also gave her prophetic instruction that saved her and her entire household: "Get up and go, you and your household, and sojourn wherever you can, for the LORD has called for a famine, and it will come on the land for seven years" (2 Kings 8:1).

Elisha essentially told the Shunammite woman to leave Israel to escape the coming famine. She understood all too well the truth we find in 2 Chronicles 20:20: "Believe His prophets, and you shall prosper" (NKJV). The Shunammite woman did not hesitate to believe and act on the words of the prophet. She took her family to the land of the Philistines for the duration of the famine—and they lived. During those years the Shunammite woman never forgot that Elisha declared she would have a son—and that the Lord brought the prophet's word to pass. She never forgot when the prophet raised her son from the dead with an appeal to heaven. So when the famine was over, she came back to Israel to make an appeal of her own to the ruling king:

> At the end of seven years, the woman returned from the land of the Philistines, and she went forth to appeal to the king for her house and her field. Now the king was talking with Gehazi the servant of the man of God, saying, "Tell me all the great things that Elisha has done." As he was telling the king how he had restored a dead body to life, the woman whose son he had restored to life started appealing to the king for her house and her land.
>
> Gehazi said, "My lord king, this is the woman, and this is her son whom Elisha restored to life." When the king questioned the woman, she told him.
>
> So the king appointed to her an official, saying, "Restore all that was hers and all the proceeds of the field from the day that she abandoned the land until now."
>
> —2 Kings 8:3–6

The Power of an Appeal

The word *appeal* in 2 Kings 8:3 comes from the Hebrew root word *tsaʿaq*, which means to cry, cry out, call, cry for help, make an outcry, cry aloud, or summon. This is not merely a request. An appeal denotes a sense of urgency—and it gets God's attention.

This same Hebrew word is used in several other scriptures that reveal the power in an appeal. For example, when Abel's blood was *crying out* from the ground, the word *tsa'aq* was used (Gen. 4:10). God heard that appeal. Before the Israelites were delivered from the bondage of Pharaoh, they *tsa'aqed* to God (Exod. 5:8). God heard that appeal. Moses appealed to God for Miriam's healing from leprosy (Num. 12:13). God heard that appeal. When Judah was under attack from the front and the back, they appealed to heaven (2 Chron. 13:14). God heard that appeal.

Psalms records several appeals to heaven based on this Hebrew word *tsa'aq*. David says, "The righteous *cry out*, and the LORD hears, and delivers them out of all their troubles" (Ps. 34:17, emphasis added). Asaph wrote, "I *cried out* to God with my voice, even to God with my voice; and He listened to me" (Ps. 77:1, emphasis added). This is a powerful appeal to heaven: "Then they *cried unto* the LORD in their trouble, and He delivered them out of their distresses" (Ps. 107:6, emphasis added).

In legal terms, *Black's Law Dictionary* defines an appeal as a complaint of an injustice done or error committed by an inferior court. The appeal aims to have a higher court reverse the lower court's decision. Drawing a spiritual parallel, you might say that when there's injustice in the natural realm—when evil is seemingly prevailing over good—you can still make an appeal to heaven. And God will hear your appeal.

Of course, not every appeal is immediately answered. Just as going through appellate courts in the natural realm can take years, some appeals to heaven demand persistence. Others are answered swiftly. The timing of the answer is not up to us. I believe in this hour it is going to take a day-and-night, night-and-day appeal to heaven akin to the persistent widow's petition to the unjust judge in Luke 18:1–5:

> He told them a parable to illustrate that it is necessary always to pray and not lose heart. He said: "In a city there was a judge who did not fear God or regard man. And a widow was in that city. She came to him, saying, 'Avenge me against my adversary.'
>
> "He would not for a while. Yet afterward he said to himself, 'Though I do not fear God or respect man, yet because this widow troubles me, I will avenge her, lest by her continual coming she will weary me.'"

We have an adversary, the devil, from which we need justice. Unfortunately we have allowed the enemy to gain an advantage over the American church and the United States as a whole. We've allowed the enemy to lull us to sleep through weariness, apathy, compromise, or blatant sin. But when the church wakes up and makes an appeal to heaven, God will hear our *tsa'aq*. Deliverance may not come overnight, but our appeal to the King will elicit a heavenly response.

Consider Jesus's conclusion to His parable in Luke 18:6–8:

> And the Lord said, "Hear what the unjust judge says. And shall not God avenge His own elect and be patient with them, who cry day and night to Him? I tell you, He will avenge them speedily. Nevertheless, when the Son of Man comes, will He find faith on the earth?"

If Queen Esther could make an appeal to the king and find justice, why can't we? If David could make an appeal to the King for mercy, why can't we? If sinners could cry out to Jesus for healing and deliverance—and miracles—why can't we? We can—and we should. We should make an appeal to heaven regarding the injustices in our lives—but we should also make an appeal to heaven over our cities, states, and nations.

Everlast and Evergreen

The revelation of making an appeal to heaven as it relates to taking back our nation for God unfolded to internationally recognized author and Bible teacher Dutch Sheets through several prophetic encounters over the course of about twelve years. Today his revelation is igniting fires of revival and awakening in the United States and beyond. Many, including myself, believe that it relates directly to a Third Great Awakening in America.

One of those prophetic encounters was a dream a young man shared with Dutch. In the dream Dutch was a boxer facing five giants in five rounds. One by one he knocked out those giants with a single punch, alternating fists. One of the boxing gloves said "Everlast," which is a common brand name for boxing gloves but nevertheless prophetic. The other glove said "Evergreen." Dutch knew God was talking to him about taking out the giants in America. "When I look at the giants in America, I get overwhelmed," Dutch says. "I have to get my focus off the giants and get my focus on the Lord. He can do this. This is not too hard for God."[1]

Dutch talks more about this in his book *Appeal to Heaven*, but the foundation of the revelation is in the Everlast and Evergreen dream—and then tied back into Scripture. As Dutch studied the life of Abraham, he was fascinated by Genesis 21:33: "Abraham planted a tamarisk tree in Beersheba, and there he called on the name of the LORD, the Everlasting God." This is the first time in Scripture that Jehovah is called "Everlasting God."

The law of first mention is a principle for interpreting God's Word that states the first mention or occurrence of a name or subject matter in the Bible establishes a pattern that is unchangeable in God's mind throughout Scripture. Until Genesis 21:33 Abraham knew Jehovah as Adonai, El Shaddai, and Yahweh. After walking through twenty-five years of struggles and mistakes waiting to see the promise of Isaac fulfilled, Abraham saw Jehovah as the "Everlasting God," or Olam-El, the strong, eternal God who fulfills the past and precedes us into our future. The Everlasting God is the one who stood by Abraham even when he lied about Sarah being his sister. The strong, eternal God is the one who stuck with him through the mess he made with Hagar and Ishmael. Olam-El is the God who delivered on the promise through faith despite it all.

"God is not finished with America—He's not," Dutch says. "God is not going to send awakening to America because we deserve it. He is not going to send awakening based on our merits or our goodness. I'm not asking for revival because we haven't sinned or because we're perfect. I'm asking for this based on His mercy and His faithfulness and the fact that He's bigger than our mistakes. And I'm asking based on the blood of Jesus."[2]

That's the revelation of the "Everlast" glove in the prophetic dream. The revelation of "Evergreen" wouldn't come until six years later at a Christ for the Nations graduation when Dutch asked one of his spiritual sons, a military man, to offer the graduation message. Long story short, the soldier pulled out a flag that George Washington flew on his naval ships before the United States of America was ever birthed. It was the banner America was born under—a white banner with an evergreen tree and the words "Appeal to Heaven" written in block letters across the top. The tamarisk tree that Abraham planted in Genesis 21:33 is an evergreen tree.

We'll explore the significance and prophetic implications of this Appeal to Heaven flag in-depth in the next chapter. But here's the bottom line as Dutch saw it: "I realized what God was saying to me is if we're going to defeat the giants, we can't be asking for God to deliver America just so we can prosper. We're going to have to tap into His eternal purpose. This is not about being the most powerful nation or the richest. This is about being that city on a hill. This is about furthering the gospel. This is about what God wants to do not just here but all over the world. We're going to have to tap into this synergy of the ages. We are going to have to do the same thing they did. If we wear the ever-lasting covenant glove and wear the evergreen covenant glove and reconnect to our roots in Him, God will come through for us."[3] That's where you say "amen."

The Enemy Doesn't Fight Fair—but God Is Just

Of course, a Third Great Awakening in America is not going to come without intercessory prayer to wake up—and stir up—the sleeping giant that is the church. The devil is a dirty fighter—and he's just as subtle as he is dirty. He never sleeps or slumbers, but over decades he worked to meta-phorically put much of the Western church to sleep through apathy, complacency, and waves of weariness.

Let's look back before we prophesy our future. Satan has been working since the Second Great Awakening to put the church back into a deep sleep. He had some stops and starts. The Azusa Street Revival, the birthplace of the modern Pentecostal movement, revived the saints at the beginning of the twentieth century. We saw the latter rain movement, the voice of healing movement, the Jesus people movement, the charismatic movement, the Brownsville Revival, and other fires burn over the years, but that slumbering spirit nevertheless crept back in unawares. And this time seems worse than the last.

In some ways the Western church is like a modern-day Samson, seduced and lulled to sleep by devilish Delilah and losing its power to combat the enemy's onslaught. Of course we haven't really lost our power. But by compromising with the spirit of the world, too many soldiers in the army of God have effectively and willfully taken off their armor and laid down their weapons because it's more comfortable to sleep through the noise of sin that's erupting all around us. A defeatist mentality has settled in among many, hope is failing, and faith is waning as the world grows darker and persecution against Christians rises.

How deep is the sleep? Many in the church have taken off the belt of truth and embraced lies that it's OK to practice homosexuality or to neglect prayer or to have sex with people to whom you're not married. Many in the church have set down the sword of the Spirit, which is the Word of God, and picked up pornography. Many others have traded church service for occultic entertainment like Harry Potter or danced to the demonic beats of modern music into the wee hours of the morning in secular clubs downtown.

Many in the church have taken off the breastplate of righteousness, compromising who they are in Christ to avoid conflict in the workplace—or in the church, or even in the pulpit. Too many parishioners laugh at dirty jokes to fit in with their worldly friends instead of being salt and light in the darkness. Too many pastors preach a sugarcoated message to keep tithes up. Too many believers have traded their shoes of peace for the trendy designer sandals of the season while neglecting to bring an offering to God. Oh, sure, many are still wearing helmets of salvation, but they sometimes wish they could hide that hat because they don't want to seem uncool in a contemporary society that shuns Christ.

Much of the church is playing the harlot—forsaking the Bridegroom for sin. Harlotry was ultimately Samson's downfall. The Bible says Samson went to Gaza and saw a harlot there and had sex with her (Judg. 16:1). Samson was literally sleeping with the enemy as he followed the passions of his flesh rather than the God he was consecrated to serve.

Then he met Delilah, with whom he fell in love—but her motives toward him were not pure. The rulers of the Philistines—who were enemies of Israel—each offered her eleven hundred pieces of silver if she could persuade Samson to share the source of his great strength so they could overpower him, bind him, and afflict him (Judg. 16:4–5). She asked Samson time and time again, and he lied to her time and time again, foiling the enemy's plans to capture him until finally she wore him down and he told her the truth.

This is a key strategy of the enemy. Daniel 7:25 reveals that the adversary wearies the saints, but the good news is those who wait on the Lord shall not grow weary (Isa. 40:31). Samson didn't wait on the Lord. He allowed the enemy's words to press him "so that his soul was vexed to death" (Judg. 16:16, NKJV). This is what we do many times—we allow the enemy's persistent words to vex our hearts until we don't feel like fighting back. We don't think we can win.

After she got what she wanted from Samson—just a little compromise—Delilah was able to lull him to sleep on her knees. He was sleeping so deeply that a man came in and shaved off seven locks of his hair. When the Philistines broke in, he thought he could break free as in times past—but he was deceived. "The Philistines seized him and gouged out his eyes. They took him down to Gaza, bound him with bronze chains, and he ground grain in prison" (Judg. 16:21).

Samson compromised. Samson was lulled to sleep by his enemy. Samson was left completely blind. That's the condition much of the church is in today. But there is good news. We can pray for another great awakening. We can pray that God will wake us up and give us another chance. We can pray as Samson did:

> Lord GOD, remember me, I pray! Please strengthen me just this once, God, so that I may get full vengeance on the Philistines for my two eyes!
> —JUDGES 16:28

Samson repented, then rose up to defeat the enemy of his nation with a prayer and a faith-filled action. If Samson—who was sleeping with the enemy—can repent and rise up in the name of God, so can we. It starts on our knees, making an appeal to heaven for a compromising nation that needs to turn back to God. God is merciful and just and true to His Word. If we make an appeal to heaven laced with humility and repentance, God will bow His ear to us and heal our land. I just know He will.

Prophesying to America's Dry Bones

God will avenge His elect who make a day-and-night appeal to Him. He will deliver those who cry out to Him steadfastly. He will respond to those who summon Him. Even though the spiritual condition of our nation is desert dry,

God can empower us to prophesy to those dry bones and see a mighty army rise up in His name with His Word by His Spirit and combat the evil forces that have threatened to steal the destiny of a generation.

Let Ezekiel's experience in the valley of dry bones inspire you to start prophesying life over America and making an appeal to heaven:

> The hand of the LORD was upon me, and He carried me out in the Spirit of the LORD and set me down in the midst of the valley which was full of bones, and He caused me to pass among them all around. And there were very many in the open valley. And they were very dry. He said to me, "Son of man, can these bones live?"
>
> And I answered, "O Lord GOD, You know."
>
> Again He said to me, "Prophesy over these bones and say to them, O dry bones, hear the word of the LORD. Thus says the Lord GOD to these bones: I will cause breath to enter you so that you live. And I will lay sinews upon you and will grow back flesh upon you and cover you with skin and put breath in you so that you live. Then you shall know that I am the LORD."
>
> So I prophesied as I was commanded. And as I prophesied, there was a noise and a shaking. And the bones came together, bone to its bone. When I looked, the sinews and the flesh grew upon them, and the skin covered them. But there was no breath in them.
>
> Then He said to me, "Prophesy to the wind; prophesy, son of man, and say to the wind: Thus says the Lord GOD: Come from the four winds, O breath, and breathe upon these slain so that they live." So I prophesied as He commanded me, and the breath came into them, and they lived and stood up upon their feet, an exceeding great army.

Then He said to me, "Son of man, these bones are the whole house of Israel. They say, 'Our bones are dried up, and our hope is lost. We are cut off completely.' Therefore prophesy and say to them, Thus says the Lord GOD: Pay attention, O My people, I will open your graves and cause you to come up out of your graves and bring you into the land of Israel. Then you shall know that I am the LORD, when I have opened your graves, O My people, and brought you up out of your graves. And I shall put My Spirit in you, and you shall live, and I shall place you in your own land. Then you shall know that I the LORD have spoken and performed it, says the LORD."

—EZEKIEL 37:1–14

The United States of is like a valley of dry bones that spans 3.8 million square miles.[4] Our nation's moral fabric is decaying from coast to coast. We have strayed so far from our Christian heritage that a president of the United States actually proclaimed that we are no longer a Christian nation.[5] And yet there is hope. We can still make an appeal to heaven. We can still prophesy to these bones that once held upright a nation built on Judeo-Christian values and biblical principles of government.

Let us rise up as an exceedingly great prayer army with hope and faith in the truth recorded in 2 Chronicles 7:14—that if God's people will pray, He will heal our land. And then let's expect God to move. Let us prophesy breath from the four winds on what remains that it may live again for the glory of God. Let us appeal to heaven as our Founding Fathers did when they set out to establish a nation that honors Jesus Christ as Lord. If God did it once, He can do it again.

Chapter 3

OUR FIRST APPEAL
TO HEAVEN

GENERAL GEORGE WASHINGTON's colonial army was slowly dying off to starvation and disease in the bitterly cold winter at Pennsylvania's Valley Forge in 1778—just over two years after the United States of America proclaimed its independence from Great Britain and its king. The fledgling nation was at war.

After two high-profile losses in Brandywine and Germantown and a strategic misstep that saw the British army occupy Philadelphia, public opinion was turning against Washington.[1] The only hope for victory—or for surviving the harsh conditions, for that matter—was a heavenly intervention.

In a letter to Governor George Clinton, an American soldier and statesman and one of the Founding Fathers of the United States, Washington wrote: "For some days past, there has been little less than a famine in camp. A part of the army has been a week without any kind of flesh, and the rest three or four days."[2] The colonial army often dined on rice and vinegar by day and shivered through the cold by night. With their bloody, frostbitten feet wrapped in rags, the soldiers could easily be tracked by the trail of blood they left behind in the snow.[3]

Many troops died from the conditions at Valley Forge. Many deserted the colonial army during that harsh winter when makeshift log cabins and campsite fires weren't enough to warm the hands—much less the spirits—of downtrodden troops facing sure defeat at the hand of a powerful, well-supplied British army.[4]

It could have been the end of the American Revolution, but Washington was a praying man who made appeal after appeal—after appeal—to heaven. Washington also had the faith to believe God would answer. See, Washington had a history with a miracle-working God that had delivered him from the hand of the enemy more than once before. Washington experienced Jehovah's saving power during the French and Indian War at the Battle of Fort Duquesne in 1755. There his clothing was tattered with bullets and two horses were shot dead while he was riding them. Washington's response: "I was saved by the miraculous care of Providence."[5]

Arnold Friberg's painting of Washington in uniform kneeling in prayer beside a white horse at Valley Forge has come to symbolize the American spirit. And William Johnson's book *George Washington, the Christian* offers insight into Washington's prayer life by offering a history of the appeals to heaven he recorded in a prayer journal. Here is one of them:

> Almighty God, and most merciful father, who didst command the children of Israel to offer a daily sacrifice to thee, that thereby they might glorify and praise thee for thy protection both night and day; receive, O Lord, my morning sacrifice which I now offer up to thee; I yield thee humble and hearty thanks that thou

has preserved me from the dangers of the night past, and brought me to the light of this day, and the comforts thereof, a day which is consecrated to thine own service and for thine own honor. Let my heart, therefore, Gracious God, be so affected with the glory and majesty of it, that I may not do mine own works, but wait on thee, and discharge those weighty duties thou requirest of me; and since thou art a God of pure eyes, and wilt be sanctified in all who draw near unto thee, who doest not regard the sacrifice of fools, nor hear sinners who tread in thy courts, pardon, I beseech thee, my sins, remove them from thy presence, as far as the east is from the west, and accept of me for the merits of thy son Jesus Christ, that when I come into thy temple, and compass thine altar, my prayers may come before thee as incense; and as thou wouldst hear me calling upon thee in my prayers, so give me grace to hear thee calling on me in thy word, that it may be wisdom, righteousness, reconciliation and peace to the saving of my soul in the day of the Lord Jesus. Grant that I may hear it with reverence, receive it with meekness, mingle it with faith, and that it may accomplish in me, Gracious God, the good work for which thou has sent it. Bless my family, kindred, friends and country, be our God & guide this day and for ever for his sake, who lay down in the Grave and arose again for us, Jesus Christ our Lord, Amen.[6]

Our First "American" Flag

About three years before Washington rallied wearied troops at Valley Forge—a turning point in the Revolutionary War—he launched a private navy carrying a flag that symbolized the American spirit. This flag preceded both the stars and stripes Betsy Ross sewed together as the "first official United States flag" released in 1776 and the yellow-and-black "Don't Tread on Me" flag depicting a snake that also emerged in 1776 on Commodore Esek Hopkins' fleet.[7]

In 1775 George Washington's "secret navy," as many have called it, flew a white flag with an evergreen tree in the middle and the words "An Appeal to Heaven" written across the top in bold black letters.[8] Just as Moses delivered the Israelites from the bondage of Pharaoh, Washington set out to deliver the patriots from the tyranny of Britain by the hand of God. Facing the reality that a battle against the mighty British army was too great for the fledgling colonial forces, Washington would not stop petitioning Providence until he saw what he believed was God's will done in the United Colonies of North America.[9]

Washington was drawing from the philosophy of John Locke, a British philosopher whom many credit with publishing works that serve as the foundation of modern philosophical empiricism and political liberalism. He authored *Two Treatises of Government*, at first anonymously, in 1689 after King James II was overthrown as part of what history calls the Glorious Revolution. Here are Locke's words from his *Second Treatise of Government* from which Washington drew inspiration for his appeal to heaven:

> The old Question will be asked in this matter of *Prerogative*, But *who shall be Judge* when this Power is made a right use of? I Answer: Between an Executive Power in being, with such a Prerogative, and a Legislative that depends upon his will for their convening, there can be no *Judge on Earth*: As there can be none, between the Legislative, and the People, should either the Executive, or the Legislative, when they have got the Power in their hands, design, or go

about to enslave, or destroy them. The People have no other remedy in this, as in all other cases where they have no Judge on Earth, but to *appeal to Heaven*. For the Rulers, in such attempts, exercising a Power the People never put into their hands (who can never be supposed to consent, that any body should rule over them for their harm) do that, which they have not a right to do. And where the Body of the People, or any single Man, is deprived of their Right, or is under the Exercise of a power without right, and have no Appeal on Earth, there they have a liberty to appeal to Heaven, whenever they judge the Cause of sufficient moment. And therefore, tho' the *People* cannot be *Judge*, so as to have by the Constitution of that Society any Superiour power, to determine and give effective Sentence in the case; yet they have, by a Law antecedent and paramount to all positive Laws of men, reserv'd that ultimate Determination to themselves, which belongs to all Mankind, where there lies no Appeal on Earth, *viz.* to judge whether they have just Cause to make their Appeal to Heaven.[10]

A Spiritual Army Rising Up

Although Locke writes in Old English that makes it cumbersome for modern readers to digest, the overarching concept is this: when a people group has submitted itself to government rulers who have power to enact and enforce laws—and when those government rulers fail to protect the rights of the people or fulfill their duty to promote citizens' well-being and make a remedy for the nation's ills—the only remaining option is an appeal to heaven.

Put another way, when the government becomes tyrannical and overrides the will of the people who elected its officials—when the government acts according to its own determination rather than considering the voice of the majority—the only thing the people can do is pray to God for justice. Although Locke's philosophy pointed to taking up arms as Washington did in the American Revolution, this twenty-first-century appeal to heaven points to taking up spiritual arms in a war that begins on our knees.

Rather than hoarding ammunition and waving Commodore Esek Hopkins's "Don't Tread on Me" flag, a spiritual army has determined to be strong in the Lord and in the power of His might, putting on the whole armor of God described in Ephesians 6 so that we can stand against the wiles of the devil who has been systematically working to destroy America. This spiritual army understands that:

> Our fight is not against flesh and blood, but against principalities, against powers, against the rulers of the darkness of this world, and against spiritual forces of evil in the heavenly places. Therefore take up the whole armor of God that you may be able to resist in the evil day, and having done all, to stand. Stand therefore, having your waist girded with truth, having put on the breastplate of righteousness, having your feet fitted with the readiness of the gospel of peace, and above all, taking the shield of faith, with which you will be able to extinguish all the fiery arrows of the evil one. Take the helmet of salvation and the sword of the Spirit, which is the word of God.
>
> Pray in the Spirit always with all kinds of prayer and supplication. To that end be alert with all perseverance and supplication for all the saints.
>
> —EPHESIANS 6:12–18

The Root of Awakening in America

As we prepare our hearts to make an appeal to heaven, it's important to remember that the United States of America was born out of the First Great Awakening and founded on Judeo-Christian principles.

In his book *The Great Awakening: Documents Illustrating the Crisis and Its Consequence* Perry Miller, a late Harvard University professor, wrote:

> "The Declaration of Independence of 1776 was a direct result of the preaching of the evangelists of the Great Awakening." Eddie Hyatt, an author, historian, revivalist and Bible teacher, confirms that our nation emerged out of a great spiritual awakening and that all the Founding Fathers, to one degree or another, were impacted by this awakening.
>
> "James Madison, the fourth president and chief architect of the American Constitution, was trained at a college that was known as a center of spiritual awakening," explains Hyatt. "Only a few years before Madison enrolled in the College of New Jersey—which is now Princeton University—Samuel Davies received a letter, dated April 16, 1757, from Samuel Finley, a trustee of the college. Finley wrote, 'Our glorious Redeemer has poured out His Holy Spirit upon the students at our college. The whole house was a Bochim (place of weeping). Mr. William Tennant, who was on the spot, says that there never was, he believes, more genuine sorrow for sin and longing after Jesus.'"[11]

According to Hyatt, the Great Awakening brought positive cultural change to colonial America. Profanity, vulgar living, and drunkenness almost completely disappeared, and entire communities were transformed. What's more, he explains, missionary work and other humanitarian enterprises were birthed. Hyatt notes colleges such as Princeton, Columbia, and Hampden-Sydney were established to equip ministers to serve new congregations. And Kings College, now known as Columbia University, opened in 1754 with an advertisement in New York papers declaring, "The chief thing in this college is to teach and engage children to know God in Jesus Christ and to love Him and serve Him in all sobriety, godliness, and richness of life with a perfect heart and willing mind."[12]

Hyatt chronicles how America's Christian heritage, birthed out of the First Great Awakening, influenced culture for the first one hundred fifty years of the nation's existence. He points to historic references from this period, including a recent ten-year study project to discover where the Founding Fathers got their ideas for America's founding documents. The study revealed that the single most-cited authority in their writings was indeed the Bible.

History of the United States, a book historian and physician David Ramsay published in 1816, pointed out that the Founding Fathers "wisely judged learning and religion [Christianity] to be the firmest pillars of the church and commonwealth."[13] And in 1820 at the two-hundred-year anniversary celebration of the pilgrims' landing at Plymouth, Massachusetts, Senator Daniel Webster highlighted America's overt Christian foundation:

> Finally, let us not forget the religious character of our origin. Our fathers were brought hither by their high veneration for the Christian religion. They journeyed by its light, and labored in its hope. They sought to incorporate its principles with the elements of their

society, and to diffuse its influence through all their institutions, civil, political, or literary. Let us cherish these sentiments, and extend this influence still more widely; in the full conviction, that that is the happiest society which partakes in the highest degree of the mild and peaceful spirit of Christianity.[14]

God Made America Great

Our Founding Fathers didn't make America great. God did. Alexis de Tocqueville, a French sociologist and political theorist, made this conclusion after an exhaustive study of American institutions that began in 1831. De Tocqueville set out to determine how America rose to greatness so rapidly after the American Revolution. Noteworthy is the fact that de Tocqueville came to America during the Second Great Awakening.

In his book *Democracy in America*, de Tocqueville wrote, "The religious atmosphere of the country was the first thing that struck me on arrival in the United States."[15] It struck him, in part, because of the contrast to his homeland. In France there was a distrust for religion, and the French Revolution actually worked to drive the church out of the public square. It was quite the opposite in early America, where the First Amendment worked to protect the government from restricting religion, specifically Christianity.

Hyatt points to a statement that has historically been attributed to de Tocqueville and quoted many times. He says it is likely that someone heard this statement in one of his many speeches and wrote it down for posterity. According to this unknown source, de Tocqueville said:

> I sought for the greatness and genius of America in
> her commodious harbors and her ample rivers—and

it was not there...in her fertile fields and bound-
less forests—and it was not there...in her rich
mines and her vast world commerce—and it was not
there...in her democratic Congress and her match-
less Constitution—and it was not there. Not until I
went into the churches of America and heard her pulpits flame with righteousness did I understand the
secret of her genius and power.[16]

In 1892, Hyatt concludes, the US Supreme Court completed
a ten-year investigation in which thousands of historical documents were investigated concerning the historic roots of
the nation. After citing more than sixty historic precedents,
the Court unanimously declared, "There is no dissonance in
these declarations. There is a universal language pervading
them all, having one meaning. They affirm and reaffirm that
this is a religious nation...this is a Christian nation."[17]

Although some elected officials—or even our president—
claim that America is not as Christian nation, we're still a
Christian nation at our root. Even if a 2014 Pew Research
study shows that the United States is on the verge of
becoming a minority Protestant country,[18] we're still a
Christian nation at our core. Even if anti-Christ agendas,
from militant atheism to gay marriage to legalized drugs to
radical Islam, are rising in America, we're still a Christian
nation at our foundation. With everything facing us in this
hour, no politician or pastor can save us. Our only hope is
to make an appeal to heaven—and it's a hope worth putting
our confidence in.

Chapter 4

THE SYNERGY OF
THE AGES

I NEED YOU to agree in prayer with Gordon Lindsay." Dutch Sheets was startled when he heard the Lord speak those words to his heart. His first thought was, "Lord, he's been dead for thirty years. I can't agree with Gordon Lindsay."

Gordon Lindsay is widely considered the steward of the voice of healing movement that was birthed in the 1940s and lasted through most of the 1950s. Lindsay's magazine, *The Voice of Healing*, chronicled and documented a supernatural revival of healing and miracles.

Healing evangelists such as William Branham, Oral Roberts, A. A. Allen, and Jack Coe spearheaded a move of God that impacted many Christians who are still fervently praying for the next move of God today. David Edwin Harrell, author of *All Things Are Possible: The Healing & Charismatic Revivals in Modern America*, described the historic outpouring as a "signs-gifts-healing, a salvation-deliverance, a Holy Ghost-miracle revival."[2] The movement revived Pentecostalism and full gospel preaching and led to the formation of organizations like the Full Gospel Business Men's Fellowship and schools such as Oral Roberts University.

Lindsay, the spiritual son of healing evangelist John G. Lake, renamed the organization Christ for the Nations when the movement shifted into something more evangelistic, with figures such as Billy Graham bringing in the harvest at stadium events across America. The apostolic ministry eventually included Christ for the Nations Institute (CFNI), a Bible school that since 1973 has set a revival fire in the hearts of many youth, including Dutch Sheets.

The Holy Spirit wanted Dutch to agree with the prayers of this great man of God who died suddenly during a time of worship at CFNI in 1973. But why did the Lord want Dutch to reach back in intercession to align with a past generation? What the Lord said to Dutch next unlocked a revelation that is vital in our day: "His prayers are not dead, and I need you to come into agreement with what I promised him. Until this generation comes into agreement with what I promised, I can't do it for him."[3]

Notice the Lord didn't say, "I won't do it for him." The Lord said, "I can't do it for him." Big difference. Before we go any further, let's dig into what Lindsay was believing God for so that you can see how vital that prophetic direction was in this hour. Of course, we don't know everything he prayed for, but we do know this about Lindsay: prayer was at the center of everything he did and the baseline for the supernatural work in the voice of healing movement.

A Band of Intercessors

In 1970, just three years before he went on to glory, Lindsay published a book called *Praying to Change the World*. In that book he shares how the Lord had been speaking to him about raising up a band of people who would make prayer a business in their lives—men and women who would pray not only until their lives were changed, but also until the world around them was altered. Based on Hebrews 7:25, which talks about Jesus ever making intercession for the saints, Lindsay believed the highest ministry in the church is the ministry of intercession. He wrote:

> Prevailing prayer is the one means that will change the world. The prayer of faith is the power that can move mountains of opposition. It is the force that can break the group of the powers of darkness oppressing millions in our land. Intercessory prayer is the means that can spare our nation the horrors of an atomic war. Determined prayer by faithful prayer warriors can make possible the successful gospel invasion on foreign fields. And as for the intercessor himself, he who makes prayer a business, will be able to look back, at the end of the years, and have the certain knowledge that his life has been a successful life.
>
> Some years ago, God spoke specifically about this calling out a world prayer band. Now we are setting forth the things that the Lord revealed at that time, with the purpose of persuading men and women to enlist in this great prayer army.
>
> One of the first things that the Lord called attention to, was that in Apostolic days, there was a regular hour of prayer established. "Now Peter and John went up together into the temple at the hour of prayer, being the ninth hour" (Acts 3:1, KJV). And that before God's people came together in unity, as the perfected body of Christ, it is necessary that they enter into a covenant of prayer...
>
> Moreover, the Lord said that He had a plan for all the people of God. To enter into that plan, they must pray, as it were, without ceasing. In so doing they will

pray into His plan and Divine will. When they have done this, they will not only get their own prayers answered and see a great harvest of souls, but they shall find that Romans 8:28, with its "All things work together for good to them that love the Lord," will become a reality in their life...

Again the Lord showed us the opposition that the forces of darkness would exert against those who prayed, and how people must not become discouraged, but press in with all their strength. Also that God would have us enlarge our prayers to include more than our own immediate sphere. He would have us learn to pray "Thy kingdom come" instead of "our kingdom come." Only such a prayer can change the world...

The devil must be dethroned. His citadels, principalities and powers must be overthrown. The saints of God must invade the heavenlies. They must do it now. We must have a great world prayer band that is praying daily for deliverance. Prayer that will build up a wall against the powers of the Antichrist, whose hour too is approaching fast... We must pray that the kingdoms of this world will become the kingdoms of our Lord and Saviour Jesus Christ. We must pray that we be true over comers. We must win the battle in our hearts, in our own homes. We must pray revival upon our own land; pray it on the heathen masses abroad... We must overthrow the powers of darkness in the heavenlies. It must be done now. For this is our hour! Mighty, dynamic, prevailing prayer will change the world of our time.[4]

The Power of Synergy

Gordon Lindsay was a hero of the faith. He was a hero of intercession—one of many throughout history. He didn't see the fullness of the prophetic promises he received, many of which he shared in his book *Praying to Change the World*. But that doesn't mean the prayers he prayed went to the grave with his flesh and bones. Lindsay's spirit is still alive, and so are his prayers—and many promises for revival are waiting to be fulfilled.

This is scriptural. In his sermon titled the "Synergy of the Ages" Dutch looks to Hebrews 11. The chapter points to men and women of God who acted in faith, people such as Abel, who offered to God a more excellent sacrifice than Cain; Enoch, who never tasted death; Noah, who built the ark; and Abraham, who waited for the city that has foundations whose builder and maker is God. Hebrews 11:13 says, " These all died in faith not having received the promises, but having seen them from afar were assured of them, embraced them, and confessed that they were strangers and pilgrims on the earth."

But the Bible doesn't stop its heroes of faith chronicles there. Isaac, Jacob, Joseph, Moses, Rahab, Gideon, Barak, Samson, Jepthah, David, Samuel, and the prophets are also listed in Hebrews 11. Despite many miracles—and despite much persecution—these faith heroes didn't see everything God promised them. Hebrews 11:39-40 says, "These all have obtained a good report through faith, but they did not receive the promise. For God provided something better for us, so that with us they would be made perfect."

"They didn't receive the answer to the promise—but they're still heroes of faith," Dutch explains. "The writer of Hebrews explains why—because they can't be complete without you. The word for 'perfect' in Hebrews 11:40 is 'complete.' In other words, God can make a promise to somebody fifty years ago, one hundred years ago, four hundred years ago, knowing He's not going to do it in their lifetime. He plans to do it through their kids or grandkids or great-grandkids because God doesn't see the bloodline disconnected the way we do. He sees it all connected and it is connected. In fact, there's nothing you can do about it. You inherited some things from Adam."5

When God told Dutch that He couldn't do for Gordon Lindsay what He promised until Dutch came into agreement with his prayers, the Lord also said something else: "I need the synergy of the ages." Dutch admits that he didn't understand that statement at first. Although he believed it and understood the concept of synergy, he didn't have full revelation on what the Lord meant.

Merriam-Webster's dictionary defines *synergy* as "the increased effectiveness that results when two or more people or businesses work together."6 Practically speaking, it works like this: if I can lift one hundred pounds and you can lift one hundred pounds, together we can lift more than one hundred pounds because of the law of synergy. In other words, the whole is greater than the sum of its parts. If you mix flour, water, and yeast and heat them together, you get a loaf of bread.

Scripturally we have a number of references for this. We know that if one can put a thousand to flight, two can put ten thousand to flight (Deut. 32:30). And did you know the Greek word for "work together" in Romans 8:28 is *synergeō*, from which we get our English word *synergy*?

In context this verse reads, "He who searches the hearts knows what the mind of the Spirit is, because He intercedes for the saints according to the will of God. We know that all things work together for good to those who love God, to those who are called according to His purpose" (Rom. 8:27–28). All things work synergistically when we: (1) love God, (2) are called according to His purpose, and (3) pray in the Spirit. The synergy of loving God, pursuing His purpose, and praying His will causes all things to ultimately work out for our good.

Jesus taught us about the power of agreement in Matthew 18:19: "Again I say to you, that if two of you agree on earth about anything they ask, it will be done for them by My Father who is in heaven." Dutch understood this principle as it applies to agreeing with the person next to him—but he didn't know he could agree in prayer with the generation or generations behind him. "Finally, the revelation of the synergy of the ages came to me very strongly," Dutch says. "I realized God is so into honoring what He did yesterday and those gone before. He actually made them dependent on us and us dependent on them. God connects the generations."[7]

Praying for the Promises

Many in Bible history had faith in God for promises they never saw manifest in their lifetime—but that doesn't make the promise null and void. God wants to connect the generations. God wants us to agree with the prayers of Gordon Lindsay, Jonathan Edwards, John Wesley, Daniel Nash, Abel Clary, and many others who contended for revival in this nation.

Nash and Clary served as faithful intercessors for revivalist Charles Finney.[8] Finney was an attorney-turned-preacher in the early 1800s, declaring he received "a retainer from the Lord Jesus Christ to plead His cause."[9] During his preaching days in New York, several revivals broke out and spread like wildfire. Finney was one of the first to allow women to pray in public. He was passionate about evangelism, had a mind for social reform, and goes down in history as a catalyst for the Second Great Awakening.[10]

Nash and Clary were what I call old-school intercessors—intercessors who rose up long before the Pentecostal church was born—whom many credit with laying the foundation of the Finney-inspired revivals. Although Finney's name is recorded in Christian history, fewer know anything about the dedication of Nash and Clary. Thankfully we can still learn plenty from these mighty men of God if we dig deep enough into their prayer lives. We can learn what it means to be a true intercessor—and we can learn to value the gift of intercession and the people who walk in an anointing to pray without ceasing and open the door for God's will on earth. And we can agree with their prayers.

Christ for All Nations President Daniel Kolenda explained that Nash would precede Finney's arrival in a city for revival meetings. He was known to stay in his room for days at a time, interceding. Weeping and groaning could be heard coming from his room. Nash would not quit until he felt that the spiritual atmosphere had been prepared for Finney's arrival.

"The greatest moves of God in American history occurred during this season of time. Entire regions were changed as a result of Finney's ministry," Kolenda says. "Historians point to those meetings as having such a profound impact upon people and societies that the effects could still be seen a century or more later. The powerful preaching of Charles Finney that saw hundreds of thousands of people saved would have never had the impact it did had it not been for the spiritual partnership with the intercessory ministry of Daniel Nash. It is interesting to note that only four months after Daniel Nash's death, Charles Finney left the itinerate revival ministry to pastor a church. The powerful revivals that characterized his ministry and changed a nation began to wane."[11]

Abel Clary was just as able with intercession. Clary traveled with Finney everywhere Finney went. Finney himself wrote of Clary, "Mr. Clary continued as long as I did, and he did not leave until after I had left. He never appeared in public, but he gave himself wholly to prayer."[12] As history tells it, Finney found Clary's prayer journal after Clary went on to glory.[13] Recorded within its pages were the chronicles of the prayer burdens the Lord put on his heart. It's no accident or coincidence that those prayer burdens aligned, one by one, with the order of the blessings poured out on Finney's ministry and the people who came to his meetings.

In chapter 12, "Making an Appeal to Heaven," we'll look at some of the prayers of intercessors and revivalists from past generations and get into agreement with them. What I hope to do right now through these testimonies is stir you up to "do it again." The Hebrew word for *testimony* actually doesn't mean to say again, but to do again. Dutch believes that if we testify about what God did yesterday, the same power will be released today. If we say it again, God will do it again!

Dutch has much more teaching on the synergy of the ages, the ancient path, and the appeal to heaven, and I'd recommend that you pick up those resources so you can hear his heart—and hear the Holy Spirit in it.[14] The Lord is confirming this spiritual principle to others, like Jennifer Miskov, a revival historian and founding director of Destiny House, a ministry designed to cultivate a community of worshippers who fulfill their own destinies and also help release in others healing, blessing, and breakthrough into destiny.

Tapping Info Wells of Revival

The moment she stepped through the doors, Miskov felt a powerful shift. She had just walked more than a mile in the below-freezing weather and entered into what she could only describe as a sacred place—the church on Attwell Drive in Toronto, home of the Toronto Blessing. She says she could almost feel the weight of the thousands of testimonies that had been shared there over the past twenty years—and the atmosphere was pregnant with hunger for God's presence.

"Thousands of people had journeyed to the church to renew their spirits and to be touched the way they had been touched twenty years ago when this historic revival started," Miskov says. "In the twentieth anniversary celebration and in several of the meetings over the following week, one of the recurring themes that continued to emerge is that there is a huge tsunami wave of revival approaching."[15]

In many ways, Miskov says, John Wimber paved the way for the Toronto Blessing. Miskov grew up in the Anaheim Vineyard church that Wimber once led. Signs and wonders was all she ever knew growing up. Seeing healings and miracles were normal for her. She always loved to hear stories about how the Holy Spirit broke out in the early days of the Vineyard movement from those who were there.

"While in Toronto, I was reminded of a story I heard about Jesus People movement preacher Lonnie Frisbee. John Wimber had invited him to preach on a Sunday night on Mother's Day in 1980. Toward the end of his talk, Frisbee had all those under thirty years old come up to the front to receive a blessing from the older generation," Miskov says.[16]

"Then he said, 'Let the power of the Holy Spirit come.' When he said this, the Holy Spirit came powerfully. From eyewitnesses, I heard that when he lifted up his hands in a *V*-shape and invited the Holy Spirit, people in a *V*-shape, according to where his arms pointed, fell over in the Spirit. From that moment on, the Holy Spirit broke out in a powerful way and the Vineyard movement of churches was launched. This movement would later birth many of the leaders in the Toronto Blessing."[17]

As a revival historian, she noticed some similarities between the Toronto Blessing that began in 1994 under John and Carol Arnott's leadership and the Welsh Revival that began in 1904 under Evan Roberts's leadership. Both movements made room for freedom in the Holy Spirit, valued and created space for the power of the testimony, and were marked by worship and seeking the glory of God.

"Since the Toronto Blessing has some roots in Lonnie Frisbee's influence, his catalytic prayer is important," Miskov says. "That Mother's Day when the Holy Spirit moved powerfully in Wimber's church, Frisbee also prophesied of another wave coming. If now, over thirty years after that prophecy, we are expecting a greater wave than ever before, why not go back even further into digging the wells of revival? Why not tap into even greater momentum than the already powerful 20 years of sustained revival that the Arnotts have stewarded so well within the Toronto Blessing? Why not go back 110 years and not only synergize Frisbee's catalytic prayer but also tap into a prayer that comes from a similar and powerful movement in Wales?"[18]

During the Welsh Revival, Miskov explains, Roberts received a download from the Lord of a certain prayer to send ahead of him to the towns where he was going to minister. Miskov relates how Roberts gave the children in those towns directions to pray this prayer in preparation for the services.

"Many times before he had even arrived, revival had already broken out. Without becoming ritualistic or creating a dependency upon a prayer, I want to invite you to access the legacy, heritage, and testimonies embedded in this prayer so we can pull from not only 20 years but from 110 years of revival history," Miskov says. "We need more momentum in the Spirit than just the 20 years for what's coming next. So rather than only pray 'Come, Holy Spirit,' which I regularly hear, why not take this prayer one step further? Why not also pray for an increase of the momentum of the tidal wave that we are inviting to come? Why not pray like both Lonnie Frisbee and Evan Roberts and ask for the Holy Spirit to come in greater power for Jesus Christ's sake?"[19]

What is that prayer Roberts sent ahead of the Welsh Revival in 1904? "Send the Spirit now, for Jesus Christ's sake. Send the Spirit now powerfully, for Jesus Christ's sake. Send the Spirit now more powerfully, for Jesus Christ's sake. Send the Spirit now still more powerfully, for Jesus Christ's sake."[20] Amen.

Chapter 5

GATHERING THE GENERATIONS

Long before I met Rick Curry, lead pastor at King's Way Church in Pensacola, Florida, and chairman of the board of the Sentinel Group, I heard about a "genuine revival" sweeping across the Florida Panhandle. Many told me the well of revival in Brownsville was uncapped and spilling over with streams flowing beyond Pensacola and across the northern part of the state in what was being called the Gulf Stream Revival.

Of course, I'd heard of revival sparks flying here and there over the years, but too often it was more hype than hope. As I continued receiving reports about true and potentially sustainable revival in north Florida, I decided to make the nine-hour drive to a meeting in Fort Walton Beach to check it out for myself.

Before the meetings I had dinner with the man and his wife whom God used to spark the revival in the region: Rick and Jennifer Curry. Over dinner this humble man of God shared with me how he had been laboring for thirty years in ministry to see what he was beginning to see now.

This precious couple shared with me how God had united pastors from various denominations in the region to awaken the church, save the lost, heal the sick, and more. They explained how the Holy Spirit was giving them a blueprint for a model of revival in which no one man or one church owned the move of God—but every man and every church could participate, lead worship, preach, pray, and prophesy according to the will of God.

I had never seen anything like it. And it all started with a prophetic dream Rick had a year before. In this rest of this chapter Rick shares his dream in his own words.[1] Let these words inspire your heart—and spur you to tap into the synergy of the ages.

FROM GENERATION TO GENERATION

I was approaching a building that reminded me of an era that long ago faded into the woodwork of our history. It was a nondescript building, quite plain. Its splendor was in its simplicity, and something about it was luring me to come in and explore. Upon entering, I noticed immediately the building seemed draped with darkness, as if it had just been closed up and abandoned. The darkness felt heavy, yet hope filled my heart as I felt something once lost would soon be recovered. I sensed that generations had walked across this building's threshold, and here they would walk again.

Immediately I searched for a switch to turn on some lights. My left hand raked down the wall. I followed the wall to my left, becoming more intrigued with every step. When I reached the end of the wall, which seemed incredibly long, a warm and gentle-spirited man suddenly appeared. He greeted me kindly. I asked him if he knew where a light switch was, and he told me the building had no electricity. However, he said, the walls were constructed with large wooden panels, and he told me I could open them to allow light and wind to blow into the room. Finding the first panel, I pushed it open slowly. It was much larger than I had supposed. I propped it open. Then I turned to look into the room, and I realized the room was considerably larger than I supposed. I would soon find out it was much, much larger.

I opened the second and the third panels, each side by side along the wall. While opening the third window, I was suddenly aware that wind was blowing into the room. Light began to flood in as well. I could hear in the distance a sound that was strangely muffled but that demanded I listen to its roar. The sound would become tremulous and the wind would become invigorating to me throughout the dream. I could now see at the opposite end of the room a massive platform, and I determined the room appeared to seat tens of thousands of people.

I continued along that wall until I reached a far-back corner, and I noticed what appeared to be massive risers as if for a great group of observers or maybe a choir. Finally, upon completing the task of opening the windows all around the room, I was utterly shocked at the size and the scope of this ancient place. The building was rustic and plain, yet it seemed beautiful in every way. The wind was blowing into the building with such force, it felt to me as if life itself was returning to this simple and grand place. The structure reminded me of an old tabernacle like the ones that held great camp meetings or healing crusades. It was utterly inspiring.

My bones seemed to respond to the ever-increasing volume of the sound. It was noise, but it was not. It was penetrating yet pleasant. It was remarkable yet indefinable. The sound was increasing with great intensity. It sounded as if the whole world were summoning the wind with a united moan—not painfully but deliberately serenading the place in which I was standing.

Unsure of the source of the sound or the significance of the wind, I stood at the front of the massive hall. I saw now that indeed it would seat tens of thousands, maybe as many as twenty-five thousand or even thirty thousand people. I stood alone, but not for long. The elderly gentleman approached me again. Seeing him much more clearly now, I found his countenance to be as endearing as his voice and his company as welcoming as his gestures of kindness.

He approached me and asked if I would like to see what would happen next. I quickly affirmed. I could hardly wait. He gestured toward the platform and placed a single chair near the leading edge of the massive stage. As we made our way up to the stage, I noticed the simplicity of the stage, but it had a large and arching bridge extending from one side to the other at the rear of the platform.

With the gesture of his hand he invited me to be seated in the chair. I sat all alone gazing upon the room, the stage, and the open windows. I can hardly describe the sound as I sat there. It continued to get louder and louder as if it were coming my way. I would come to believe the sound was the gathering of generations, each carrying upon the wind their mighty anthems of praise.

THE PILGRIMS, PURITANS, AND PIETISTS

Suddenly movement outside the window to my immediate right caught my attention. I leaned forward and saw ancient ships pulling into a beautiful harbor outside the building. The ships docked and people began to disembark, and the sound was overwhelming. The people were dressed very conservatively, and it appeared all of them were wearing black. I asked the man, "Who are these people?" He replied, "These are the Pilgrims, the Puritans, and the Pietists."

I watched as they made their way to the old auditorium where I was seated alone. They filed in and formed neatly defined rows, never acknowledging my presence at all. They were singing! They were singing in harmony with the sound of the wind that was rushing through the building. The Pilgrims, Puritans, and Pietists continued filing in methodically, filling every seat and every row beginning at the front of the auditorium. They were sitting right in front of me.

After filling the seats, a great number of them rose up and went to the rear of the auditorium to sit in the choir risers. It was incredible. They sang beautifully, ancient songs I had never heard. They sang in a dialect and a cadence that was remarkable. There was a prophetic sound released in their song. Then they sat down as one.

THE PIONEERS

The sound increased, and again my attention was drawn to the outside of the building. I heard the sound of horses and wagons. I looked, and I saw horse-drawn carriages, surreys, and covered coaches of all kinds pulling upon the grounds next to the building.

Children were playing, and families were coming arm in arm. The sound continued to increase, and I realized they too were singing. Their song incredibly was not conflicting in sound or scope with the song of the Pilgrims, Puritans, and Pietists. I can't explain it. It was simply as if they were singing the same song in incredibly varying ways, but it was perfectly harmonious. I felt I was for the first time watching the gathering of generations.

I asked the gentleman, "Who are these people?" He replied, "These are the pioneers. They have marked the path for those who come after. They were the visionaries and trailblazers." When they entered the auditorium, all of the previous group stood and began to release a tremendous shout of welcome! They began to twirl and dance. They began to celebrate as if they could hardly believe their eyes. It was exuberant in sound and exaggerated in joy.

Upon entering the auditorium, they began to fill row after row of seats. There were many of them! In a similar fashion, after being seated, some of them took their places in the massive choir risers at the rear of the auditorium. They were all dressed in period-specific clothing, and the massive celebration continued for some time.

THE PLANTERS

I then heard another group approaching. They were driving very early automobiles of all sorts. I saw what looked like Model As and many other types of cars pulling onto the grounds next to the auditorium. I could distinctly hear the clattering of the early combustion engines. They came singing, and though distinct from the previous two groups, their songs were blending into one thrilling anthem with the first two groups.

I asked the gentleman beside me, "Who are these people?" He said, "These are the planters. They have labored to build cities and factories of all kinds. They have built communities through building schools and churches, and many wonderful inventions have come from them."

As this group began to make its way into the auditorium, the two previous groups stood as one people and began to clap and cheer, dance and twirl around. The sound continued to increase, and it was at this point that I felt I was listening to the anthem of the ages. The song of the Spirit interpreted by the inspiring voices of each generation was being sung again in this magnificent old auditorium.

This group methodically took their seats, continuing to fill the auditorium with both people and praise. I paused to look outside the auditorium through the windows, and I was inspired by the modes of transportation that were represented, from the ancient ships in the harbor to the very first automobiles, with wagons and surreys in between.

THE PROPHETS

Suddenly I heard a distinct sound—a loud sound—of a new group arriving. I saw many cars pulling up that looked like models from the early twentieth century through the 1960s, though no specific dates were associated with any of the groups of people. This group stood out to me in the dream, as they seemed to be much more diverse and independent.

I inquired of the gentleman, "Who are these people? They look and sound different from the others." He replied, "These are the prophets. The uniqueness of their times will cause them to begin to define the world for generations to come." I have come to believe since the dream that this truly was at many levels one of the most prophetic times in all of our history to this point.

As they made their way into the auditorium, all of the previous groups stood to welcome them with song and dance. It was an overwhelming celebration. People were jumping and dancing as though they could hardly believe what they were seeing. Seated on the platform observing the scenes unfold, I felt overwhelmed by the wonderful sights.

They filed in and found places to sit as methodically as the previous groups. Just like all of the previous groups, they too had a large segment of people who went and joined the others in the large choir risers in the back. In the dream I thought this might be the last group to appear as a good bit of time seemed to pass. But then suddenly another group appeared on the scene.

THE PRAGMATISTS

I saw a commotion outside the auditorium and realized very modern and sophisticated modes of transportation began to flood onto the grounds. Modern cars were arriving, planes landing, and helicopters sounding as they battered the wind. I was fully aware of the complete spectrum of modes of transportation from ancient ships to millions of dollars' worth of sophisticated planes, trains, and automobiles.

I inquired again of the gentleman, "Who are these people?" He replied, "These are the pragmatists. They are a generation influenced greatly by reason and logic." Upon entering the auditorium, all the previous groups shouted with a voice of triumph! It was a shout unlike any shout I had heard in the dream. They found their seats after an extended time of celebration all over the auditorium. It was amazing to watch Pilgrims and pioneers dancing with each of the generations who came after them.

ARE YOU READY TO TAKE YOUR PLACE?

The gentleman instructed me to watch. He pointed toward the rear of the platform to large double doors that opened on their own. There was a large bridge that spanned the expanse of the stage. Ministers from each of the generations represented in the dream walked through the open doors and onto the arching bridge.

When they arrived at the top of the bridge, they would stop and stand facing the massive audience of the ages. A representative from each of the groups addressed the audience with a prophetic word or decree. The moment the minister would begin to speak, a great quiet would fall across the audience. Each of them carried a unique authority and released a powerful word. I recognized several of the ministers who entered the auditorium and felt amazed to be in their company.

The gentleman then gestured to me with his hand and asked a question that seemed to penetrate my spirit like an arrow. He asked, "Are you ready to take your place?" He pointed to his left, and I immediately saw a group of modern ministers walk through the door. I saw many whom I recognized and have appreciated over the years from a distance. I had never met many of them, but I knew they were in the line of powerful witnesses who, unlike the previous groups, would not only be reflecting on history but leading us forward.

As they stood at the door, one of the ministers I saw was Dutch Sheets. When I saw him, I knew I was to go line up behind him as the gentleman gestured and asked, "Are you ready to take your place?" I lined up behind Dutch without saying a word to him. We made our way up the bridge. When we arrived at the top of the bridge, Dutch extended his hand over the generations gathered in the auditorium, and a tremendous hush immediately fell across the crowd.

Dutch began to prophesy, and I noticed he began to wave a flag in a figure eight pattern. The flag was white, and I saw a large pine tree in the center of it. Further, I could see something else, possibly words written on the flag. Dutch began to prophesy about the coming harvest on the earth and a move of the Spirit that would be unprecedented in history. His prophecy was passionate and powerful. It is time for the "synergy of the ages," as Dutch says, and the reaping of the greatest harvest the world has ever known.

When we came down from the bridge and joined the other ministers on the floor of the massive stage, a spontaneous celebration broke out among the ministers and the audience. Everyone in the room was jumping, twirling about, and embracing one another. It was a glorious celebration!

Suddenly the gentleman who had walked with me through the entire dream stepped up to a pulpit that was now placed at the center of the stage. Silence pierced the atmosphere, and all listened intently. He began to speak of the days ahead. He began to declare that God's people would return to the ancient path—the way of holiness—and a mighty harvest would be reaped throughout the nations of the earth. Millions would soon rush into the kingdom, and the world would begin to see in ways no one living has ever seen the manifest glory of God sweep across the earth reaping a mighty harvest and releasing many signs, wonders, and miracles. Things are about to change in a dramatic way.

When He Woke Up

When Rick woke up, he had many questions for the Lord, but his immediate curiosity revolved around the flag Dutch was waving. When he told his wife, Jennifer, about the dream, they started googling to see if there was a flag that matched the one he saw in his dream. His jaw dropped when he found the Appeal to Heaven flag online and read about its historical significance.

Rick had no idea that Dutch had recently received the Everlast-Evergreen revelation that I shared in chapter 2. Rick didn't even know Dutch personally at the time. But when Rick shared his dream with Dutch, it served as further confirmation that God remembers His covenant with America and His heart longs to answer the prayers of the Pilgrims, Puritans, Pietists, pioneers, planters, pragmatists, prophets, and many others through the generations who have made an appeal to heaven for the United States of America. It's time to tap into the synergy of the ages. Are you ready to take your place?

Chapter 6

EVANGELISTS MOVE ON AMERICA

JONATHAN EDWARDS. CHARLES Finney. John Wesley. Charles Spurgeon. George Whitefield. Billy Sunday. Dwight L. Moody. American history is peppered with radical revivalists who carried strong words for a blessed nation.

Who could forget the words that woke up the masses? "Although believers by nature, are far from God, and children of wrath, even as others, yet it is amazing to think how nigh they are brought to him again by the blood of Jesus Christ," said Whitefield, an English open-air preacher who helped take the Great Awakening to Britain and was known in his day as the "marvel of the age."[1]

Whitefield's sermons spurred listeners toward salvation even as Billy Sunday, a nineteenth-century professional baseball-player-turned-evangelist, declared decades later, "A revival does two things. First, it returns the Church from her backsliding and second, it causes the conversion of men and women; and it always includes the conviction of sin on the part of the Church. What a spell the devil seems to cast over the Church today!"[2]

The list of inspirational—and convicting—quotes from men and women of God in decades past fills books. Their sermons saw masses come to Christ in the 1700s and 1800s during the First and Second Great Awakenings. Since then we've seen the Pentecostal movement, the voice of healing movement, the Jesus people movement, the charismatic movement, the prophetic movement, the apostolic movement, and other revival fires burn. But none of these movements have produced societal transformation.

In fact, as I noted in the first chapter of this book, our society has been on a slippery slope headed toward the spiritual avalanche that the late evangelist Steve Hill prophesied about since the US government took prayer out of schools in 1962. We won't review the statistics here, but it didn't take long to notice the decline of Christian values in our nation.

Despite the warnings, Christianity in America has strayed from its biblical roots—and biblical teachings—even as the church fights within itself over who's right about doctrines on spiritual gifts and prosperity. The church has largely turned inward, preferring the comfort of movie night and Sunday potluck within its four walls over spreading the gospel in local communities.

This is not an idle criticism. According to a Barna Group study, only half of born-again Christians say they actually shared the gospel at least once in a year with someone whose beliefs were different in hopes the person might accept Jesus Christ as his Savior.[3] Yet at a time when it seems evangelism is going out of style, God has sent fiery evangelists to the United States to blow the trumpet of salvation with the sense of urgency found in the Edwardses, Finneys, Wesleys, Spurgeons, Whitefields, Sundays, and Moodys of past generations.

"All America Shall Be Saved"

One of the most notable evangelistic voices rising up in our land hails from Germany and has spent much of his adult life ministering in Africa. Indeed, Reinhard Bonnke is best known for his crusades in Africa and for his cry, "All Africa shall be saved!" More than 55 million Africans came to Christ under his ministry from 2000 to 2009 alone,[4] and some 74 million people have made decisions for Christ during his thirty-five years of preaching.[5] Now Bonnke is declaring, "All America shall be saved!"

Widely known as the Billy Graham of Africa, Bonnke moved to the United States to begin making evangelistic films. Bonnke worked with Universal Studios and Lucas Films to create the eight-part Full Flame Film Series that he hoped would light a fire in Christians around the world to engage in Holy Spirit–led evangelism. With the films he also created study materials to equip viewers to win souls. Bonnke has moved the headquarters of his ministry, Christ for All Nations (CfaN), to the United States and is now an American citizen.

"I always thought God had sent me [to America] for the sake of preaching the gospel in Africa," Bonnke says. "But the Lord spoke to my heart and said, 'I did not just send you to America for America to be the offering plate to Africa. I've sent you to America for the sake of America. She also needs the gospel desperately.'"[6]

Ordained in 1964, Bonnke is no stranger to hard spiritual climates—or to seeing the glory of God overcome those environments. He first started working as a missionary in Africa at the age of twenty-seven. His first fellowship meeting in Lesotho attracted a hundred people, but his audiences quickly grew until they filled an entire stadium. During the 1980s he preached to crowds of 75,000 in Cape Town and 150,000 in Malawi, eventually peaking at 1.6 million at a crusade in 2000 in Lagos, Nigeria.[7]

"We have seen God do so many mighty things in Africa," he says. "But I know that He is the same God, and He will shake America. America shall be saved. America will be saved, and this is the day of salvation."[8]

Make no mistake; Bonnke's eyes aren't closed to the problems in America. He sees the rise of same-sex marriage and mourns the millions of abortions. He sees the discouragement and is aware of the economic issues. He hears the doom and gloom from prophetic voices and the negativity from the news media. But he's not giving an ear to that.

"This is not the day of damnation; this is the day of salvation," Bonnke says. "Do you know what Satan hates about us as human beings? He hates the image of God in us. He wants to remove it and replace it with his own image. He's got a big sledgehammer, and he tries to flatten the Spirit of God. So many people suffer under those hammerings of sin, and they don't know how to help themselves."[9]

CfaN President and CEO Daniel Kolenda says there is only one thing that can remove the spiritual darkness that has engulfed America. The United States, he says, will be saved only through a massive outpouring of the Holy Spirit. "I see the seeds of a movement of evangelism and the Holy Spirit that will sweep across the nation from sea to shining sea," Kolenda says. "Our nation is in desperate need of revival. The solution won't come from the White House, and it won't be fixed through the polls. It will only come from Jesus."[10]

Bonnke and Kolenda are traveling across the United States drawing tens of thousands to stadium events to hear the gospel. They plan crusade after crusade after crusade and believe God is able to bless America with salvation like never before. Bonnke is not looking into the past. He's looking into the future—and he sees the gospel as America's future.

"I am scanning the skies for men and women who pray and weep for the salvation of America. As Bill Bright used to say, 'Let's leave our logos and egos.' Let's rally at the foot of the cross of Calvary and preach the Gospel of salvation to the nation," Bonnke says. "The Holy Spirit will cooperate. God is pouring out His Spirit with glorious indifference to our differences! He said, 'I will pour out of my Spirit on all flesh.' And it seems to me He pours Himself into the mold of any vessel."

Billy Graham's Big Hope

Many years ago Ruth Graham was reading a draft of a book her husband, the beloved evangelist Billy Graham, was writing. Graham recalls that when his wife finished a section describing the terrible downward spiral of our nation's moral standards and the idolatry of worshipping false gods such as technology and sex, she startled him by saying, "If God doesn't punish America, He'll have to apologize to Sodom and Gomorrah." He wonders what his late wife would think of America if she were alive today.[12]

Indeed, America's moral decline is nothing new. As far back as 1966 Graham called for a return to the Bible as the authoritative guide for national life during a message to the American Bible Society (ABS). In that speech an impassioned Graham pointed to what he called "one of the greatest tragedies of America" in that day: millions of Americans weren't reading the Bible.[13]

The problem has only grown worse since Graham's speech. Only 43 percent of survey participants in the 2014 "The State of the Bible" report from ABS and Barna Group could name the first five books of the Bible. That's probably partly because Bible ownership has decreased over the past two decades. While 79 percent of Americans cite the Bible as a holy book or sacred literature, only 46 percent read it more than a couple times a year. As this percentage has eroded, so has our society.[14]

"America is facing a moral crisis that will ultimately determine the future of this nation," Graham said in his 1966 message. "The security of America is not being threatened abroad so much as it is being threatened by immorality at home. We are in the midst of a moral struggle that is just as important for the survival of America as the revolution led by George Washington and his co-patriots."[15]

A year before the infamous Summer of Love in 1967 that sparked a so-called hippie revolution, Graham noted that moral confusion is nowhere more apparent than in the area of sexual morality. He warned that the country is paying a "fantastic price" for this moral-sexual confusion and is "getting worse with every passing hour." Graham went so far as to say that this confusion threatened the foundations of our democracy and the security of our republic—and he probably never saw the gay marriage push coming. Few likely understood just how prophetic were his words fifty years ago.[16]

"We are rapidly becoming a secularized society," Graham warned. "We are unwittingly accepting the idea that man is simply a physical being—that life on this planet is all there is. This materialism and secularism has captured millions of people in Europe and America. Millions now explain the universe without a reference to God, morality without the Ten Commandments, personality without a soul, the good life without hope of immortality. This is blatant secularism and humanism."[17]

Fast-forward five decades, and Graham is trumpeting this message: America needs our prayers more than ever. Although he's nearly a century old, Graham still prays for America—and he's praying fervently for a fresh spiritual awakening in the nation. "If ever there was a time this country needed the intervention of God, it is now," Graham says. "We can and should pray for America as a whole, but remember that when God sets out to change a nation, He begins by changing people. It starts with individuals."[18]

As Graham sees it, the further we get from God, the more the world spirals out of control. "My heart aches for America and its deceived people," he says. "The wonderful news is that our Lord is a God of mercy, and He responds to repentance. In Jonah's day, Nineveh was the lone world superpower—wealthy, unconcerned, and self-centered. When the Prophet Jonah finally traveled to Nineveh and proclaimed God's warning, people heard and repented."[19]

The Evangelist of the Future

Dubbed the "evangelist of the future" by Billy Graham, Greg Laurie celebrated twenty-five years of evangelistic outreach in Southern California during the 2014 SoCal Harvest. Founded by Laurie and the late Chuck Smith in 1990, Harvest Crusades have drawn millions of people to stadium events across the country and around the world. All told, Laurie, who is also senior pastor of Harvest

Christian Fellowship—one of the largest churches in the United States—has shared the gospel message with more than 6.5 million people around the world at events and via live Internet productions.[20]

"As we look at our country right now, I think we could agree that it is going downhill fast with the moral and spiritual breakdowns in our nation. So can a country ever turn around again?" Laurie asks. "I hope we all have gotten the memo that the solution is not political. No politician from any party will be able to turn this country around. Our primary problem is spiritual, and the only solution for turning our nation around is spiritual. That will come as a result of people praying."[21]

Laurie believes America has two options before her: judgment or revival. If we don't have a revival, he says, then we are in big trouble in the United States. Like many in this hour, Laurie is pointing to the great harvest that came during past great awakenings and thanks God for what He did then. But this is what he's praying: "Do it again, Lord."

"That needs to be our prayer, that God would do it again. We need another Great Awakening, another revival, another Jesus Movement," Laurie says. "The prophet Habakkuk understood this when he prayed, 'I have heard all about you, Lord. I am filled with awe by your amazing works. In this time of our deep need, help us again as you did in years gone by. And in your anger, remember your mercy' (Habakkuk 3:2, NLT). The psalmist prayed, 'Will You not revive us again, that Your people may rejoice in You?' (Psalm 85:6, NKJV)."[22]

To this Southern California evangelist—the evangelist of the future—revival means to bring back to life again, an invasion from heaven. He describes revival as when God is at work and you can't explain it. That is what he wants to see again: a revival that we can't explain how it started, but where people are packing out churches, coming to Christ, and praying.

"The secular culture doesn't need revival; they need evangelism," Laurie says. "And here is the interesting thing: Evangelism doesn't necessarily produce revival, but revival always produces evangelism. Whenever there has been an awakening, there has been an evangelistic thrust that has come as a result. When God's people are awakened, when they are restored, when they are revived, then they go out and start doing what they should have been doing all along, which is proclaiming the gospel. I pray that the church will have revival. And I pray that our culture will hear the gospel."[23]

A South African Targets America

South African evangelist Rodney Howard-Browne, founder of Revival Ministries International and pastor of The River at Tampa Bay church, is on a mission to see another Great Awakening in America—and in the nations of the earth. His Great Awakening tour and broadcast have spanned 101 countries and 3,871 cities to see more than 10.5 million souls come into the kingdom.[24]

"Soul-winning is not a program, it's a passion, and it has to start in the pulpit and go to the pews," Howard-Browne says. "And when everybody in the pew is mobilized, from the littlest child to the oldest saint, that's when we're going to start seeing the harvest come in."[25]

The Great Awakening Tour is not another Christian conference. It's a radical campaign to reach a radical generation that impacts their communities with the life-changing message of Jesus Christ. Howard-Browne has always been passionate about soul-winning, but when his eighteen-year-old daughter died of cystic fibrosis on Christmas morning 2002, he and his wife, Adonica, made a vow that the devil would pay for what he had done to their family. They are laboring to win 100 million souls to Jesus and put $1 billion into the harvest—and America is a major focus.[26]

The problem in America, he says, is that everything has become a formula and the goal is to cater to the needs of the people with latte makers in the lobby and a Disney World–type experience. By contrast, he says, in China fifty people are sitting cross-legged on a damp cement floor sharing a single Bible. It boils down to a lack of spiritual hunger. When things are desperate, he says, you have to turn to God.

"I don't think the American church is ready for what's coming because the preachers are preaching each other's sermons; they are prophesying each other's prophecies. People are asleep at the wheel," says Howard-Browne. "The only thing we can do is bring in the harvest of souls. This is not about a government bailout. The government cannot change what's coming…We've got to see a revival. We've got to see a Great Awakening."[27]

So How Do We Evangelize?

There is no lack of evangelism training in the body of Christ. CfaN has training resources for believers who want to do the work of an evangelist. Laurie and many others hold stadium crusades to which you can invite your friends. Billy Graham's My Hope campaign lets you introduce unsaved friends and family to Jesus in your living room. But Howard-Browne, a walking, talking definition of evangelist, trains believers to share the gospel in seven practical steps:

1. Start by asking a question; e.g., "Has anyone ever told you that God loves you and has a wonderful plan for your life?"

2. Follow this with the key question: "If you were to die this very second, do you know beyond a shadow of a doubt that you would go to heaven?"

3. Present the gospel. Share verses such as Romans 3:23, Romans 6:23, and Romans 10:13, and keep it simple—no Christianese! Remember, the power is in the gospel. You are putting the pressure on God's Word to touch their hearts, not your persuasive words.

4. Pray for them. Don't ask if you can—chances are more likely they'll say no—but boldly say, "I'm going to pray a quick prayer for you." Then say something like, "Lord, bless [name] and his family with long and healthy lives. Jesus, make Yourself real to him and do a quick work in his heart. If [name] has not received You as his Lord and Savior, I pray he'll do so now."

5. Give them the opportunity to pray with you; e.g., "If you'd like to receive the gift God has for you today, say this after me..." Then pray the sinner's prayer with them; e.g. "Jesus, I ask You to come into my heart. Forgive me of my sin. Wash me and cleanse me. Set me

free. Jesus, thank You that You died for me. I believe that You are risen from the dead and that You're coming back again for me. Fill me with the Holy Spirit so I can live for You."

6. Encourage them. Let them know that what they just prayed has given them a new life and that their sins are truly forgiven.

7. Connect them. Invite them to your church or get their contact information so you can follow up with them.

Howard-Browne reminds us that on the Day of Pentecost the fire fell to bring in the harvest. The same power is available to us today. Jesus said, "But ye shall receive power, after that the Holy Ghost is come upon you: and ye shall be witnesses unto me both in Jerusalem, and in all Judaea, and in Samaria, and unto the uttermost part of the earth" (Acts 1:8, kjv).

"A witness is a demonstrator, somebody who's willing to die for what he believes," Howard-Browne notes. "So when we walk into town as witnesses, we don't just speak a dead word, but we actually demonstrate by His power that He is alive. The same power that rolled away the stone is right there with us."[28]

Chapter 7

TRANSFORMING REVIVAL
IS TRULY POSSIBLE

F OR NEARLY TWO hundred years Clay County, Kentucky, was marked by violent family feuds, moonshining and murder, extreme poverty, government corruption, and deadly drug abuse. Clay County—and specifically the city of Manchester—made national headlines over and over again for all the wrong reasons.[1]

In the early 1990s there were reports that over 40 percent of Clay County's population was growing marijuana and the Daniel Boone National Forest was effectively being transformed into a pot field.[2] By the turn of the century the area moved on to a new drug of choice. The *Lexington Herald-Leader* dubbed Manchester "The Painkiller Capital of America" in 2003, as OxyContin was sold on nearly every street corner.[3] From there "cooks" and crooks rose up to manufacture methamphetamine, a highly addictive crystalline drug that can be snorted, smoked, or injected.

Public officials and police were being paid to look the other way. The drug lords bought the elections every four years. Over 90 percent of the county's high school students were strung out on one drug or another. Overdoses became a common occurrence, with so many memorial crosses strewn along the city streets they looked like a picket fence. Meanwhile the pastors were polarized based on doctrinal differences and felt hopeless to help members whose families were drug-addicted and dying.

"Our kids started dying. Out of desperation we started praying in the fall of 2003. We started crying out to the Lord," says Doug Abner, who was pastoring a church in Manchester at the time. "A Southern Baptist preacher named Ken Bolin had a dream. Ken wanted to have a march against drugs and corruption on May 2, 2004. We received threats on our lives, our homes, and our churches, but we knew it was God."[4]

The morning of May 2, in the pouring rain, four thousand people turned out for the march. That's especially significant considering Manchester is home to only two thousand people. The rally ended at a park. There the pastors and church leaders repented for being more concerned about their own denominations, congregations, and programs than the lost souls in Clay County. When they asked the people to forgive them and vowed to work together, Abner says the manifest presence of the Lord fell in the park to the degree that people could hardly breathe.

"The fear of the Lord gripped the community," Abner says. "Drug dealers and corrupt politicians began to tell on each other. A few months later the FBI came to town and started arresting people. Eventually they arrested the mayor and the assistant police chief, the fire chief, the 911 director, several local judges and city council members, a circuit judge, school board members and the superintendent, and lots of others. They arrested the drug dealers, who were selling drugs to the nation from Manchester."[5]

Today Manchester is known as the City of Hope. God even healed the land. For years the water tasted foul without a water filter. But in 2008 Clay County's water won first place in Kentucky's municipal water system for its taste. After years of streams without fish, suddenly big fish repopulated the rivers. Manchester also is now home to fishing tournaments. The forests once were barren of life, but now the bear, turkey, and elk have returned in droves. Churches and local businesses banded together with the court system to develop second-chance employment programs for Clay County's recovering drug addicts. As the economy improved, new businesses started opening to provide those jobs.[6]

"I asked the Lord, 'Why Manchester?' And He said, 'Because I want the world to see what can happen when people get desperate and begin to come together,'" Abner says. "As bad as the darkness was, our biggest problem was not the darkness. Our biggest problem was the lack of light—the church not being what it is supposed to be. When we came together in desperation, He healed the land. He changed the fabric of our society."[7]

Manchester Was Not a Fluke

Transformation is possible in America, just as transforming revival has broken out in communities around the world. The Sentinel Group, a Christian research and information agency dedicated to helping the church pray knowledgeably for end-time global evangelization and enabling communities to discover the pathway to genuine revival and societal transformation, has documented transformation in about one thousand communities worldwide.

A transformed community, as the Sentinel Group defines it, is a neighborhood, city, or nation whose values and institutions have been overrun by the grace and presence of God; a place where divine fire has not merely been summoned but has fallen; a society in which natural, evolutionary change has been disrupted by invasive, supernatural power; a culture that has been impacted comprehensively and undeniably by the kingdom of God; and a location where kingdom values are celebrated publicly and passed on to future generations.

Consider some of the accounts the Sentinel Group has documented:[8]

- For decades the city of Cali, Colombia, carried a notorious reputation as the cocaine capital of the world. No institution escaped the ruling cartel's ruthless and corrupting hand. In the mid-1990s, however, the drug lords' icy grip was finally broken when desperate believers surged into local soccer stadiums to hold all-night prayer vigils.

- The seaside village of Nateleria, Fiji, was the classic case of paradise gone wrong. No fresh water. A dead reef. A rash of youth suicides. But that was before the twelve hundred or so locals repented of their sin and rededicated their land to God. Two days later a brilliant light appeared over the coast, setting the sea ablaze for thirty minutes. When it was all over, the reef had been healed and thousands of fish were swimming in the shallows.

- With a long tradition of worshipping the devil, Karawu, Papua New Guinea, has been called the backward sister of the Keapara villages. In 2006, however, the locals took a cue from Fiji's prayer-based process to "heal the land" and burned their fetishes in deep repentance. Economic life improved almost immediately— salty water turned fresh, gardens thrived, and abundant sea life returned.

- Fischer Village, Brazil, doesn't look like much until you realize that until a few years ago most of the inhabitants were living in a garbage dump. The residents fought with vultures for scraps of rancid meat, and their constant companions were disease and death. Moved by their cries, God launched a rescue plan that has brought dramatic healings, new homes, and fresh hope.

- Almolonga, Guatemala's "Big Carrots" community was made famous by the Sentinel Group's widely distributed *Transformations* video. Formerly a town of idolatrous and drunken brawlers, Almolonga is now a bustling, Christ-centered farming center. With 85 percent of its nineteen thousand inhabitants claiming a born-again experience, the secular media have dubbed it the "*Ciudad de Dios*," which means the City of God.

- Shillong, India, is the capital of Meghalaya, one of only three Christian-majority states in India. In 1905–1906 the area experienced revival, but the fire eventually died out. A century later, local believers prayed fervently for three years that God would come again—and He did! An outpouring in 2006–2007 saw thousands converted, healed, and delivered. Distilleries closed, and children spoke forth the Word of God.

- Located in the desert region of northern Brazil, Algodão had not seen rain for twenty-three years. Only a handful of believers existed in this dying community—but as they cried out to God for help, He responded by opening the heavens. As rain poured down, the land and its people were transformed. Once described as "gray," Algodão now grows several kinds of crops and harvests fish and shrimp from a once-dry reservoir.

- Scotland's Outer Hebrides are well known for revivals, and none more so than the Isle of Lewis. Although it has now been a half century since the last notable visitation, the lingering effects of this mighty move can still be felt. Thousands were saved over the years as they came under great conviction of sin, including many sailors and fishermen on passing ships.

Scriptural Backing for Transformation

True transformation is not based on a person's opinion. Scripture offers clear indicators. The Sentinel Group offers the following ten points along with scriptures for your study as you build your faith for transformation in your community.

1. Political leaders publicly acknowledge their sin and dependence on God (2 Kings 11:17–18; 23:2–3; Jon. 3:6–9).

2. New laws, curricula, and business practices are put into effect (2 Chron. 19:4–10; Neh. 10:31).

3. The natural environment is restored to its original life-nurturing state (Lev. 26:4–5; 2 Chron. 7:14; Ezek. 34:27; 36:29–30).

4. Economic conditions improve and lead to a discernible lessening of poverty (2 Chron. 17:3–5; Ps. 144:13–14; Isa. 60:5; Amos 9:13).

5. There is a marked change in social entertainment and vices as kingdom values are integrated into the rhythm of daily life (Ezra 10:1–4; Neh. 8:10; Eccles. 10:17; Acts 19:17–20).

6. Crime and corruption diminish throughout the community (2 Kings 12:13–15; Neh. 5:6–12; Isa. 60:17–18).

7. Volunteerism increases as Christians recognize their responsibility to heal and undergird the community (Isa. 58:10–12; 61:1–4).

8. Restored hope and joy leads to a decline in divorce, bankruptcy, and suicide (Neh. 12:27–28, 43; Isa. 54:11–14; 61:3–7; Jer. 30:17–19; 31:11–13; Hosea 2:15).

9. The spiritual nature of the growing socio-political renewal becomes a hot topic in the secular media (2 Chron. 20:29; Neh. 6:16; Isa. 55:5; Ezek. 36:36; Acts 19:17).

10. Overwhelmed by the goodness of God, grateful Christians take the embers of revival into surrounding communities and nations (2 Chron. 17:9; Isa. 61:6; Acts 11:20–26).

Three Stages of Transforming Revival

Transformation doesn't happen overnight, but it doesn't have to take a lifetime either. George Otis Jr., founder of the Sentinel Group, says the one thousand communities in which he has documented transforming revival passed through three distinct stages.

Stage one—awakening

It starts with what he calls the "invitation stage." This is when people humble themselves, fast, and repent of sins.

"They re-covenant with God," Otis says. "They form unity kernels and they prevail in prayer. And with clean hearts and pure hands they ask God to rend the heavens and come down—not first and foremost to repair the community but because they cannot bear to live apart from His presence a moment longer. They are not summoning a handyman. They're summoning a lover. And when they do this, there is a certain moment in time where the presence of the Lord comes. God comes in response to that entreaty."[9]

How long do believers need to dwell in the invitation stage? It doesn't need to take long, Otis says, but it can take time because believers are carrying so much baggage. Particularly in the West, Christians have theological obstacles to overcome and distractions at every turn. Western believers would like to see revival but don't want to break stride. Or, as Otis puts it, we want revival as long as it "falls out of the sky like a pizza on our left shoulder."[10] In his experience, Christians are more excited about seeing the community transformed but less enthusiastic about being transformed themselves.

"Community transformation or corporate transformation of necessity must be preceded by individual transformation— and that's where the rub so often comes in the Western world," Otis says. "In most of the cases we've been tracking, once people really locked in and got serious with God and started to do the things that He says in His Word He will come if we do, it's generally a thirty- to ninety-day process. That happens very quickly, and when the presence of God comes in to the community it is an immediate thing. It's an instantaneous thing. It is not progressive. It wasn't there a moment before and now it is."[11]

Stage two—visitation

Otis calls the second stage "visitation." This is the shortest of the three. Otis describes it as a corrective phase that is "highly intense." During this time daily routines are put on hold as God comes in somewhat like a divine chiropractor and snaps all areas of dysfunction back into alignment. The fruit of visitation includes rapid, substantial church growth, miracles, and an overwhelming sense of the pervasive presence of God in every area of the community.

"Believers and nonbelievers encounter it," Otis explains. "In fact, there's nowhere you can go within the community where God's presence doesn't dwell—in parks, prisons, offices, taxis, schools—it's everywhere. This is hard for

Westerners to fathom because we have very rarely encountered anything like it. I have, and once you have, you never forget it. It's an amazing and remarkable thing, and it's very consistent with what we read about in Scripture and what we read about in account of historical awakening."[12]

Stage three—transformation

Of course, there comes a point where the visitation phase, also called the awakening phase, comes to an end. Otis compares it to when Jesus left the earth and told the disciples that He was sending the Holy Spirit to guide them into all truth (John 16:13).

"It's like the Lord is saying, 'This phase is over. Now keep your eyes focused on Me, and I'll show you how to steward and maintain this blessed condition that I have brought about through new business practices, new educational curricula, new legislation and statutes, and so forth so that we get into the one-hundred-year transformation experience of the Moravians,'" Otis says. "So we don't want to just ask, 'How do revivals begin?', but we want to also ask, 'Why did they end very often prematurely.' And it's because people don't transition well from this time of visitation into the longer term or time of stewardship, which is called transformation or reformation."[13]

Oftentimes, Otis says, Western Christian communities try to jump directly to that third phase of reformation with efforts to incrementally remake a society in God's image through education and political reform. He has never seen such efforts succeed, not historically or in modern times. It only works if there comes first a divine visitation.

"I call it divine hydraulics, where God comes in and does the heavy lifting that is beyond human capacity," Otis says.

"He puts things in order, and then we can steward that in all phases of society. But we can't cut out that stage and think that we can do enough. Only God can transform a community, but we can certainly be along for the ride."[14]

The First Great Awakening not only impacted the church by driving believers to repent, but it also transformed the fledgling colonial government, helped birth the United States of America, and reformed the educational system. The Second Great Awakening led to mass evangelism and birthed denominations. What the Third Great Awakening will bring remains to be seen, but our desperate appeal to heaven will open the door for God to pour out His transforming Spirit. Part of our role is to humble ourselves, repent of our sins, call out to Him in prayer—and expect Him to come.

"We've got to get Christians in the West to migrate from hope to faith and expectancy," Otis says. "It's like setting a wedding date, which is very different than an engagement. Engagement is all about hope, but once you set a wedding date, it's not about someday. It's about that day. All of a sudden you're sending out invitations. You're choosing flowers. You're choosing bridesmaids and colors. You're now on the clock. The way you live your life changes.

"We don't behave this way when it comes to transforming revival because we've got all kinds of theological hitches and inhibitions. We think maybe we're trespassing on God's sovereignty. God is desperately anxious to come. In fact, we're already late in most of our communities. Transforming revival should have happened ten years ago, twenty years ago. Because we didn't get our act together, there is that untold suffering and bondage and addiction. You have to think about it from the perspective of the victims and the lost souls within the community. They don't have the luxury of waiting for years until Christians sort of get their act together."[15]

If you are like me, Otis's words stirred your heart. I was shaken to my core, and when I hung up the phone, I started asking God what more I could do. The truth of the matter is, revival begins with me—and you. If you are burning to cooperate with God in this process right now, skip ahead to chapter 11, "Revival Begins With You." But be sure to come back to the following chapters so you can fully understand the challenges to revival and awakening, revival pitfalls to avoid like the plague, and sustaining revival unto reformation.

Chapter 8

OVERCOMING CHALLENGES TO REVIVAL AND AWAKENING

YEAR AFTER YEAR I hear the same fervent prayers rising to heaven from many denominations and movements across the body of Christ: "God, pour out Your Spirit. Send revival." And yet the outpouring we long for has not manifested. What gives? Doesn't God want to send revival? Doesn't God want to see the church wake up and rise up? Doesn't God want to see the flood of souls come into the kingdom that results from an awakening?

Why won't God answer our intercessory prayers? After all, James 5:16 says, "The earnest (heartfelt, continued) prayer of a righteous man makes tremendous power available [dynamic in its working]" (AMP). Are our prayers not heartfelt enough? Do we lack persistence? Do we lack righteousness? Does God lack the power to bring revival to our nation? Of course not! So what gives?

There's not one single reason, but there is a solution. Some of the challenges are in the culture and some are in the church. It's up to the body of Christ, though, to recognize and overcome these challenges because lives are at stake.

So ultimately, no matter how you look at it, the pulpit is to blame. Charles G. Finney, a leader in America's Second Great Awakening, recorded these words on December 4, 1843:

> Brethren, our preaching will bear its legitimate fruits. If immorality prevails in the land, the fault is ours in a great degree. If there is a decay of conscience, the pulpit is responsible for it. If the public press lacks moral discrimination, the pulpit is responsible for it. If the church is degenerate and worldly, the pulpit is responsible for it. If the world loses its interest in religion, the pulpit is responsible for it. If Satan rules in our halls of legislation, the pulpit is responsible for it. If our politics become so corrupt that the very foundations of our government are ready to fall away, the pulpit is responsible for it.[1]

Those words were true then, but they are especially prophetic for our generation. Immorality is prevailing in the land. There is a decay of conscience. The media lack moral discrimination. The church is degenerate and worldly. The world has lost its interest in religion. Satan rules in our halls of legislation. Politics are corrupt, and humanist politicians are chipping away at our Judeo-Christian foundations. True change starts with the pulpit preaching repentance, but that doesn't let the rest of the body of Christ off the hook. We all have a part to play in ushering in the next great awakening.

Do We Have Faith for Awakening?

Hopelessness has infiltrated the church. Some doom-and-gloom prophets insist there is no hope for America, pronouncing God's impending wrath without a way of escape through repentance. Again and again in the Bible we see the mercy of the Lord toward those who would turn back to Him—and even toward those who cried out to Him in the midst of judgment. Isaiah pronounced judgment over and again but is still known as the prophet of hope.

Our intercession can hold back judgment. Even though the Lord ultimately destroyed the city, Abraham's intercession for wicked Sodom paved the way for Lot's deliverance from the fire and brimstone (Gen. 18:16–32). Moses interceded for Israel when God said, "Now therefore let Me alone, so that My wrath may burn against them and I may destroy them. And I will make of you a great nation" (Exod. 32:10). And Ezekiel 22:30–31 tells a sad story that we should take to heart before we decide it's not worth praying for God's mercy over America:

> I sought for a man among them who would build up the hedge and stand in the gap before Me for the land so that I would not destroy it, but I found no one. Therefore I have poured out My indignation on them. I have consumed them with the fire of My wrath. Their own way I have recompensed on their heads, says the Lord GOD.

Joseph Matterra, founder of Mattera International Ministries, bishop of Resurrection Church in New York, and the US ambassador for the International Coalition of Apostles, offers a laundry list of modern challenges to awakening and revival. Among them are a fragmented society; entertainment distractions; affluent churchgoers; a lack of preaching on the law of God, the Ten Commandments, and heaven and hell; an absence of the fear of the Lord in churches; a failure to seek God and pray; and a gospel that's failing to permeate the elite systems and people of American culture.

"Many—if not most—evangelical and Pentecostal churches have only a lukewarm commitment to seeing the power of God operate in their midst," Mattera says. "Even in Pentecostal churches rare is the evidence of the gifts of the Spirit and healing power of God in both the church services and in people's lives."[2]

As he sees it, American and Western Christianity is bowing more and more to the mind-set of its culture, devolving into churches that offer nice programs and therapeutic messages run by corporate-style church governments and systems. In most cases, he bemoans, the simplicity and power of the gospel has been replaced by this pragmatism and naturalism.

"The average pastor and church attendee is expected to stay home when they are sick instead of going to church to get healed, and is just as likely to depend on natural remedies to cure their physiological, emotional and physical maladies as their unbelieving neighbors," Mattera says. "The expectation for God to break forth and heal, deliver and perform miracles is largely absent from Western churches. We need to recapture the awe, majesty and mystery of God again in our churches!"[3]

True Unity Is Lacking

I believe there is more than a single reason revival has not manifested, but one major culprit is division. I've long noticed a lack of unity in the body of Christ, and it has long grieved me. But the Holy Spirit has recently given me a keen awareness of the gravity of this lack of harmony. It grieves me deep in my spirit—and if it grieves me, I can only imagine how it grieves the Holy Spirit.

I don't have the space in this chapter to give you all the scriptures on unity, but I want to share one with you that really stirred my spirit recently—and I hope it will stir yours. It comes from the fivefold ministry mandate in Ephesians 4. As I read these verses, I was struck by how much we focus on equipping the saints but seem to fail to recognize what we're ultimately equipping folks to do. Read the passage for yourself and see if you catch what the Holy Spirit illuminated to me.

> And He Himself gave some to be apostles, some prophets, some evangelists, and some pastors and teachers, for the equipping of the saints for the work of ministry, for the edifying of the body of Christ, till we all come to the unity of the faith and of the knowledge of the Son of God, to a perfect man, to the measure of the stature of the fullness of Christ.
>
> —EPHESIANS 4:11–13, NKJV

We usually stop after the "equipping the saints for the work of the ministry" part. But we can equip the saints for the work of the ministry all day long, and that won't necessarily bring revival. You can't work your way into revival. The anointing will flow in our churches when we come to the unity of the faith. Sure, we may disagree on whether gifts of the Spirit have ceased or whether women can preach, but we can still unite under the Apostles' Creed.[4] And if we want revival—not just powerful meetings but sustained revival that brings true change—we must unite.

I am convinced this disunity in the body of Christ is causing more problems than we can see even with a discerning eye. I am convinced people are dying and going to hell because the church isn't walking in unity. I don't want this blood on my hands, so I am challenging you—and challenging myself—to be in one accord and of one mind (Phil. 2:2), to put on love that binds us together in perfect harmony (Col. 3:14), and to strive side by side for the faith of the gospel (Phil. 1:27) even with those who have small differences in how they view the Rapture, spiritual gifts, and other issues that aren't central to the gospel of Christ.

One huge reason we don't have revival is because strife in the church is holding back the blessing. Consider the words of the psalmist: "Behold, how good and how pleasant it is for brothers to dwell together in unity! It is like precious oil upon the head, that runs down on the beard—even Aaron's beard—and going down to the collar of his garments; as the dew of Hermon, that descends upon the mountains of Zion, for there the LORD has commanded the blessing, even life forever" (Ps. 133). Amen.

Having said that, let me offer a balancing word here. Pursuing unity doesn't mean tolerating compromise or sin in the church to avoid stirring the waters. Unity doesn't mean we ignore deeper issues that will ultimately bring destruction to people's lives. Unity doesn't mean preaching a gospel of inclusion. Unity is not letting preachers from faiths that are out of line with the gospel of salvation into your pulpit to share a message. We cannot compromise the gospel. There is no revival without repentance. Unity and repentance are baselines.

An Absence of Kingdom Thinking

In 1998 Ken Malone, founder of Forerunner Ministries in Florida, was part of a move of God in the Bahamas. For two and a half years he was involved in what he calls a "small Book of Acts revival" in the Abaco Islands. He reports that many souls came into the kingdom, and there were many healings and miracles. Malone knows plenty about what propels revival—and what hinders it. Beyond strife, which he pegs as one of the greatest hindrances to revival, he says taking ownership of what God is doing, a lack of "kingdom thinking," and unequipped churches can also be stumbling blocks.

"Taking ownership of a move of God when it is a work of the Holy Spirit is a huge hindrance," Malone says. "The ownership of revival is a result of religious pride. I remember asking a church leader to join myself and other leaders who were crying out for revival in Central Florida. The answer the leader gave shocked me to the core: 'I can't be a part because the Holy Spirit said the next revival in this region is going to come through our church.' This is called 'touching the glory.' My response was, 'I don't care what church it comes through, I want to be a part.' Revival may come through one of the least expected ways and places."[5]

When you look historically at local-church revivals, Malone notes, the latter condition of the local church is often worse than before the revival began. He believes that's because an outpouring was never meant for a local church only—but for a territory, city, or region. As he sees it, local congregations and their leaders should steward the awakening in their city.

"When you look at the Word of God, an outpouring of the Holy Spirit came on cities and regions," Malone says. "When Jesus addressed the church, He never broke it down below a city level. We first see awakening revival coming to the city of Nineveh. Transformation was the result of the Lord sending Jonah with the word of the Lord. The inhabitants of Nineveh along with their king repented in sackcloth and ashes. A real awakening will impact a city to the point [that] strip clubs close their doors, saloons have no patrons, and prostitutes and their johns are born again, forsaking their ways. Homosexuals and lesbians are saved and return to the normal desire."[6]

Malone is convinced that, for the most part, congregations are not equipped for the work of the ministry. They hear messages Sunday after Sunday and get their needs met, but what would happen if awakening revival hit and thousands came to Jesus in a matter of days? What would happen if our churches filled up literally overnight? What if new believers outnumbered the mature saints in a congregation?

"Some leaders and congregations will think they don't want to go to church with these former sinners, former drug addicts, former drug lords, former prostitutes, former homosexuals and lesbians," Malone says. "They are coming and they will have tattoos everywhere you can put one and piercings everywhere you can put a piercing. They do not look churchy. They don't look like the elders, deacons, or pastors. They will need to be discipled, equipped, and sent out into their city to minister. Equip the congregation through each of the fivefold gifts to do the work of the ministry. Then send them into their community to do the works of Jesus."[7]

A Two-Headed Monster

R. Loren Sandford, founder and senior pastor of New Song Church and Ministries in Denver, Colorado, and author of *Visions of the Coming Days* and many other books, is convinced we are coming into a new outpouring of the Spirit. Speaking with prophetic insight, he says this will not be a reliving of past revivals, nor will it be a continuation of the movements of recent decades—it will be different in ways that would be difficult to explain apart from the actual experience of it.

"I can say only that a fresh newness is coming to us who can receive it and that it will be more rooted in the Father's heart and the character of Jesus than any that have come before," Sandford says. "Be aware, however, that historically whenever there has been a fresh move of the Spirit, opposition has erupted. It comes in two forms. The first comes from those who don't really want the Spirit to move, who can't handle the mess it makes or who find their theology threatened by it. It would seem that the spirit of religion cannot allow for anything to occur that human beings cannot control or understand."[8]

Sandford learned long ago that one person's order and decency are another person's boredom and death, and that not everyone will be comfortable with the freedom revival brings. Hidden in what might appear to be chaos, he says, may be a well-established order and set of protocols. And beneath a reserved appearance someone might be having a deep and powerful experience of God.

"Realize also that it is biblically sound for God to act in ways that are unprecedented and out of the box," Sandford says. "There was, for instance, no biblical precedent for the gift of tongues on the Day of Pentecost. While Joel and others foresaw the gift of the Spirit, no passage of the Old Testament could be construed as a clear prophecy of that gift. While God will never actually contradict Scripture or act in a way not consistent with His own nature, He nevertheless 'does whatever He pleases' (Ps. 115:3, NAS), and we would be wise to make room for it."[9]

Sandford says the second form of opposition comes from those who want revival and don't mind the mess it makes but who think themselves immune to deception. Specifically in these days to come, he says, the enemy will access weaknesses and unhealed regions of the heart to twist words and perceptions in order to paint the leaders of that move of the Spirit as having less-than-pure motives or as having said abusive or inappropriate things that were neither said nor intended.

"As the words actually spoken get twisted and changed, offense will be taken, then held in the heart and fed," Sandford says. "If not actually altered, words spoken innocently and in righteousness will often be perceived in ways that distort their meaning and intent. Those who get caught in this trap will be led to believe that their 'discernment' is godly and accurate so that correction becomes exceedingly difficult and is often rejected.

"The enemy intends this to cause division and to wound and weaken leaders so that they cannot lead as effectively as God intends. Lest anyone in my own circles think I'm speaking specifically of you, know that I am in touch with pastors and leaders in many places who tell me stories that reflect the dynamic I'm articulating. It is not uncommon and comes with the territory."[10]

Sandford says this two-headed demon of opposition rises simultaneously with an increase in the move of the Spirit and blinds those caught in it to what is really going on. No one is so holy as to be immune to this. Sandford has been privileged to live through the Charismatic Renewal, the Vineyard movement, shades of Pentecostalism, and more recently the Toronto Blessing, and he says he has seen this dynamic play out every time God has launched a new thing.

"To think that you are immune to it constitutes the kind of pride that comes before a fall," Sandford says. "Don't fall prey to the enemy's strategy! Stand for oneness. Keep your heart clean. Before assuming anything about the heart of another or even what you think you understand from what you've heard or seen, ask questions and then honor the answers you receive. What's coming is glorious, but the way is narrow that leads to life."[12]

We Just Aren't Desperate Enough

I believe a fresh move of the Spirit is coming, but I believe it will take place in our response to desperation. I believe desperation is the ultimate key to overcoming every obstacle to revival. David Ravenhill, son of the late revivalist Leonard Ravenhill, has a rich history in ministry, including working with David Wilkerson's first Teen Challenge Center in New York City and the international ministry Youth With A Mission, and pastoring one of the largest churches in New Zealand.

Ravenhill believes we don't see revival because we just aren't desperate enough. He truly believes God wants to send revival to our nation, but he also believes that if we experienced revival now, the vast majority of believers would go on with business as usual.

"I well recall during the first year of our ministry working with Brother David Wilkerson in Teen Challenge in Brooklyn, New York," Ravenhill says. "One cold winter's day two drug addicts came in seeking shelter. Brother David talked to them for a while and then I saw them leave. Brother David said to me after they had left that he couldn't help them because they were not desperate enough to give up their drugs. He went on to say that all they really wanted was a bed for the night and a good hot meal. I somehow think that is what the church is looking for in revival—a good sermon, some great music, followed by some carpet time."[13]

Ravenhill points to the story of Hannah, who traveled yearly with her husband, Elkanah, to Shiloh to worship and sacrifice to the Lord (1 Sam. 1:1–15). Hannah was sorely distressed because she was barren. She wept at the altar, pouring out her soul to the Lord. She would not eat. Her heart was grieved, and her husband didn't really understand her pain. The priest Eli falsely accused her of being drunk. But she was so desperate that she kept crying out—and God answered her desperate prayer for a child by giving her Samuel.

Pastors Steve and Kathy Gray know a thing or two about what it takes to see revival—they stewarded two revivals, first the Smithton Outpouring in 1996 and then another outpouring in 2008. People from across the United States— and from seventy nations around the world—flocked to the Grays' church in Smithton, Missouri, just as they had flocked to Brownsville, Florida, starting in 1995 during the Pensacola Outpouring.

Steve Gray says it was "plain old desperation" that opened the door to God's presence. "I was determined that nothing else mattered. I didn't know what I was going to do with my life," says Gray, senior pastor of World Revival Church in Kansas City, Missouri. "I went on a desperate journey for myself. We prayed for two and a half years for the presence of God to come, and we prepared ourselves for what would happen when God's glory came."[14]

John Kilpatrick, who served as pastor of the Brownsville Assembly of God during the Pensacola Outpouring, calls it urgency. He believes this lack of urgency is a key reason we don't see revival—and that most Americans have a false sense of security. "Recently, as I was praying before preaching to our congregation, the Holy Spirit said to me, 'I have many ministers, and they are speaking on

My behalf, but there is something missing—the urgency in their voices,'" Kilpatrick says. "So many of our pulpits deliver messages that seem to be speeches or lectures and not passionate sermons that stir the church to holy living."[15]

Doug Stringer, founder and president of Turning Point Ministries International, which birthed an international movement called Somebody Cares, asks a series of pointed questions: What will it take to obtain both personal victories and breakthroughs for our cities and nation? What brings us to our knees? What causes us to cry out to God in desperation? Is it simply an unquenchable desire to draw close to the lover of our soul? Or does it take something tragic to awaken our hearts?[16]

"I believe our passion for Christ must be greater than our passion for anything else," Stringer says. "A genuine passion for Christ allows no room for compromise or mediocrity. We must come to the Lord with transparency and seek Him and His heart. As the late revivalist Leonard Ravenhill said, 'God doesn't just answer prayer; He answers desperate prayer.' God sees our need but wants us to come honestly and openly before Him with all of our fears, insecurities, disappointments and sins. When we do, He will replace our facades with His healing virtue and power."[17]

We see plenty of examples in the Bible of God answering desperate prayers. Jairus was desperate for his daughter's healing (Matt. 9:18–26). The woman with the issue of blood was desperate for her own healing (Luke 8:43–48). Blind Bartimaeus was desperate for his sight (Mark 10:46–52). All of these received what they cried out for. Throughout Scripture we find that when people cry out to the Lord in desperation, the Lord hears their cries and delivers them. It may not happen overnight, but it happens consistently. America is just not desperate enough yet. But the desperation that brings revival starts with a remnant making an appeal to heaven.

Chapter 9

REVIVAL PITFALLS TO
AVOID LIKE THE PLAGUE

SPARKED BY JONATHAN Edwards and George Whitefield, the First Great Awakening lasted from the 1730s to the 1770s. Faith was revived, church membership increased, and evangelistic efforts spread—but what caused it to end? The Second Great Awakening lasted even longer and saw the likes of Charles Finney, Peter Cartwright, and Francis Asbury take the gospel to the masses from 1790 to the 1840s—but, again, what caused it to end?

As we look back through history, we see that the Moravian revival in the 1400s, the Welsh Revival, and the Azusa Street revival in 1906, the latter rain revival in the 1940s, the healing revival in the 1940s and 1950s, the Jesus people and charismatic revivals in the 1960s and 1970s, the Brownsville and Smithton Revivals in the 1990s, the Lakeland Revival in the 2000s, and many others all started out strong but ultimately petered out. Although it's impossible to sustain revival forever, few revivals led to awakening, reformation, or transformation like what we've seen in Manchester, Kentucky, the Republic of Fiji; or other communities around the world where the land was literally healed.

"The Jesus People movement was an international work of God, but its lasting fruit was greatly diminished because of the massive lacks in the Church of the early 1970s," says Michael L. Brown in his book *A Time for Holy Fire: Preparing the Way for Divine Visitation*. "The Charismatic Renewal was another genuine move of the Spirit, but for many, gifts more than God formed the center of their experience. Therefore what could have been was not to be. Beyond these moves of the Spirit, there were genuine revivals in the past that had a real impact, but then the fire faded, the new wine waned, and only a few went on in power while the rest lived on a memory."[1]

Revival for revival's sake is refreshing, but it's not the ultimate goal. Revival should lead to awakening, and awakening should lead to transformation. So why do we see so many sparks of revival but so little lasting change in American society? Why does it look like the enemy has been successful in transforming America's once Christ-centered society into a culture marked by immorality, idolatry, murder, and all manner of sin?

Although revival cannot be sustained forever, I believe sustained transformation is realistic if an awakened people keep their eyes on Jesus. Of course, there are many roadblocks, pitfalls, and stumbling blocks along the way. But by understanding the roadblocks, pitfalls, and stumbling blocks of past revivals, we can cooperate with the Holy Spirit to see more than a refreshing wind through the church today—we can see the church fully wake up, rise up, and bring God-driven change to the nation.

"A pitfall of revival is the direct opposite of a positive characteristic that is imperative for revival. There are many of them, and often they slip in unnoticed or rendered as small and insignificant," says Rick Curry, lead pastor at King's Way Church in Pensacola, Florida, and chairman of the board of the Sentinel Group, which studies transforming revival. "Like Samson seduced through subtleties, many have lain down in the lap of compromise and paid an enormous price. The discipline is to build on the spirit of righteousness and holiness, preferring the presence of the Lord over all programs or people, and [to] walk in integrity."[2]

What Is Revival?

Before we go further, let's define some of the terms being used so you can see the difference clearly. What do I mean by revival, awakening, reformation, and transformation?

In *The Sword and the Trowel* Charles H. Spurgeon wrote this about revival:

> We are constantly speaking about and praying for a "revival;" would it not be as well to know what we mean by it? Of the Samaritans our Lord said, "Ye worship ye know not what," let him not have to say to us, "Ye know not what ye ask." The word "revive" wears its meaning upon its forehead; it is from the Latin, and may be interpreted thus—to live again, to receive again a life which has almost expired; to rekindle into a flame the vital spark which was nearly extinguished....When Christians are revived they live more consistently, they make their homes more holy and more happy, and this leads the ungodly to envy them, and to enquire after their secret.[3]

An awakening goes beyond the four walls of the church to impact the society. Lost souls are translated into the kingdom. After the Holy Spirit was poured out, Peter preached a sermon that saw three thousand men saved—that's not counting women and children (Acts 2:41). Another time Peter preached and saw five thousand men—not counting women and children—added to the church (Acts 4:1–4). During this season, Acts 2:47 says, "the Lord added to the church daily those who were being saved." This was truly the first great awakening.

Once the church is revived and society starts to awaken to the saving grace of Jesus, reformation can begin. You've probably read about the religious revolution known as the Reformation in the sixteenth century, when Martin Luther and John Calvin launched a movement that essentially birthed the Protestant Church. We still celebrate Reformation Day—the day Luther nailed his ninety-five theses to the castle church door in Wittenberg, Germany—on October 31, 1517.

Five centuries later, we need another reformation. Rather than a reformation of church theology that questions the Roman Catholic's methods of salvation, we need a reformation that transforms a corrupt, immoral society in which humanists, atheists, and others with anti-Christ agendas are working erase God from the culture. The church's failure to reform society—and our tendency to allow society to reform the church—has led us to the current state of affairs we discussed in the first chapter of this book. In biblical reformation society turns away from foreign gods and makes a conscious decision to serve the Lord. Ezra and Nehemiah were both reformers in their days. We need the spirit of Ezra in our nation even now.

Transformation is a major change—a transfiguration, conversion, or metamorphosis. This goes beyond lives or churches to institutions, industries, cities, governments, and even nations. A revival in Cali, Colombia, sparked awakening and reformation that saw the defeat of the Cali drug cartel, which the US Drug Enforcement Agency once considered "the most powerful crime syndicate in history."[4] Transformation is what we are aiming for, but we can't get there if our revivals are derailed before they have the opportunity to awaken society and drive reformation.

What Derails Revival?

Before we attempt to cooperate with God to bring revival, awakening, and reformation to our lives and our land, we need to understand what derails revival lest we press in with zeal without knowledge of how the enemy uses our own weaknesses to put out the fire of the Holy Spirit. What are the pitfalls of revival? One of the primary resisters and derailers of a new move of God is often those touched by the last move of God.

Charles Finney once wrote this:

> Now it is remarkable that, so far as my knowledge extends, all the seasons of great revivals with which the Church has been blessed from the very first, have been broken up, and the revival influence set aside, by an ecclesiastical and sectarian janglings to preserve what they call the purity of the Church and the faith once delivered to the saints. I believe it to be a truth, that ministers, as a class, have always been responsible for the decline of revivals; that their own sectarianism, ambition, and prejudice have led them to preach and contend, to run to Synods, Councils, and other ecclesiastical meetings, until the Churches at first pained, and even shocked, with this tendency of

things, have come to adopt their views, imbibe their spirit, and get entirely away from God.[5]

Spiritual pride is a derailing force for revival. Jonathan Edwards boldly declared that the first and worst cause of error that prevailed in his day was spiritual pride.

> This is the main door by which the devil comes into the hearts of those who are zealous for the advancement of Christ. It is the chief inlet of smoke from the bottomless pit to darken the mind and mislead the judgment. It is by spiritual pride that the mind defends and justifies itself in other errors and defends itself against light by which it might be corrected and reclaimed. The spiritually proud man thinks he is full of light already and feels that he does not need instruction, so he is ready to ignore the offer of it.[6]

When an outpouring happens in a single place or a single church, pride will try to find a way in to puff up preachers. But God will not share His glory with any man. In fact, J. Lee Grady, former editor of *Charisma* magazine and founder of the Mordecai Project, a ministry that confronts the global oppression of women, says the one-man show is over.

"New Testament ministry is about teams, not hotshots," Grady writes. "Paul shared the workload with Barnabas, Phoebe, Clement, Priscilla, Aquila and many others. And he protested when people tried to make him out to be a god. When will we learn that the superstar syndrome actually thwarts genuine revival because it causes audiences to focus on man instead of Jesus?"[7]

I agree and believe the next move of God will not be centered on one city or one church—or on one man. In fact, pockets of revival and awakening are already breaking out in areas across the United States with great diversity among the leadership, denominations, and manifestations of the Holy Spirit. Nevertheless, the spirit of religion still rears its ugly head.

When Religion Rears Its Ugly Head

The religious spirit—or, if you'd prefer, a legalistic mind-set—can quench and grieve the Holy Spirit all at once. Religious spirits are nefariously nasty. The spirit of religion works to murder reputations, pervert the revelation of who we are in Christ, put us in bondage to legalism, and much more. Remember this: Jesus broke many "religious" traditions.

One of the earmarks of the religious spirit is hypocrisy. People may walk in obedience to the Lord—walking in love with their brothers and sisters in Christ—until a certain point. Unless you cross that line, you'll never see their religious spirit in all its wickedness. Revival brings out the religious spirit in droves as it looks to oppose the move of God. Jesus said, "Woe to you, scribes and Pharisees, hypocrites! You shut the kingdom of heaven against men. For you neither enter yourselves, nor allow those who are entering to go in" (Matt. 23:13).

Hypocrisy is the heartbeat of the religious spirit (or mindset). Although not reserved for believers—nonbelievers can have a legalistic mind-set as well—Christians with a religious spirit are essentially working against the gospel in which they say they believe. There are some Christians who have a form of godliness but deny its power (2 Tim. 3:5). Religious spirits deny the power and grace of God to change people, and in doing so wax judgmental, self-righteous, prideful, critical, legalistic, and argumentative with fellow believers (and lost souls).

"The Spirit falls dramatically on an entire congregation, hundreds are touched and transformed, and religious believers get offended. Why? Because their sacred traditions were violated," Brown says. "The preacher didn't use the King James Bible (or, in some circles, his 'sin' was that he *did* use the King James). People jumped, or fell, or laughed, or cried; they were too loud, or they were too quiet. The service lasted for five hours, or the sermon lasted for five minutes. The sick were prayed for before the message (or, maybe there wasn't even a message). 'That's not how we do it in our church!'"[8]

We need to discern the operation of this wicked spirit in whatever form it reveals itself and resist it. Make no mistake; the religious spirit wants to keep you from entering into the fullness of the kingdom of God, which is righteousness, peace, and joy in the Holy Ghost (Rom. 14:17). And the religious spirit wants to shut out revival or kill it once it starts.

"Religious hypocrites—or shall I say *religious racists*—are dangerously close-minded," Brown says. "If the spiritual emphasis doesn't originate with their group, they categorically reject it. If the revival doesn't reflect their particular way of doing things, it can't be from heaven. And they will even *persecute* the new thing God is doing in the earth. As Paul said, 'The son born in the ordinary way persecuted the son born by the power of the Spirit' (Gal. 4:29)."[9]

Three Personal Pitfalls to Avoid

Rick Curry of King's Way Church in Pensacola outlines three personal pitfalls to avoid. He calls them the untamed heart, the undisciplined life, and the unwilling participant.

The untamed heart

In the exuberance and varied expressions of revival, he warns, we must guard against the pitfall of carrying a partial revelation out of season because of the swiftness with which we can move. As Curry sees it, guarding against this first pitfall means embracing revivals that are guided by mature fathers and mothers and wise apostles, and that are envisioned by seasoned prophets. "The untamed, wild heart is a rebellious heart," Curry explains. "The wild heart promotes self and style over substance and significance. The wild heart runs swiftly without the wisdom of history. A tamed heart is a heart rightly aligned and empowered to achieve its greatest cause and highest destiny."[10]

The undisciplined life

The second personal pitfall is an undisciplined life, which Curry characterizes as a life lived irresponsibly. A life lived irresponsibly, he says, is one absorbed in a self-confidence and pride that deceives the person into thinking his calling is greater than his actions. "It is a pitfall for all who forget that our gifts and callings along with every anointing that causes [us] to flourish is first and foremost God's gift and [is] not attributable to ourselves," Curry says. "To forget that is to be drawn into arrogance and hubris. What a pitfall it is! If an undisciplined life is a life governed by pride, then a disciplined life is to be governed by purpose. We learn to avoid the pitfall of pride by disciplining our lives to the fullness of His purpose. We learn to avoid the pitfall by walking in humility and holiness."[11]

Curry says a disciplined life marked by purpose touches the world; a life disciplined by purpose is a dreaming life, a desirable life, a life committed to integrity and purpose, a destiny-reaching life. "It is character that guards your gifts and protects your life from a trap designed to leave broken people in its wake," Curry says. "When you carry a move of God, there must be a willingness to be disregarded and written off."[12]

The unwilling participant

Finally, Curry says, the unwilling participant will not join the process of transforming revival and urges us to reject every tendency to allow other people's failures to intimidate us, lead us into indifference, or trap us in hopelessness. History, Curry says, is forever marked by ordinary men and women who encountered the manifest glory of God and then by obedience touched the world.

"Could it be that God wants to use you? Could it be that you are far more capable than you have imagined, and could it be that you possess the capacity to be one who marks the world for His glory? Yes!" Curry says. "The Lord is raising up a generation of nameless and faceless men and women who have labored for years in the secret place, but He is now unveiling them as a gift to the world—men and women not wholly perfect but [who are] willing participants."[13]

Curry sees the next decade as one that will witness the rise of a generation ablaze with the glory of God, who will do mighty exploits unlike the world has witnessed before. He sees a generation of burning ones who are willing participants in the divine strategy of God in the earth. He also believes the Lord in the next decade is going to call upon a generation of older adults to pour into those coming after them in ways we have never seen before.

"Retirement will become extinct for many, and they will run alongside a generation of radical trailblazers and pioneers," Curry says. "We are living in unprecedented times, and unprecedented times provide unparalleled opportunity. You must set your heart to become a willing participant in the move of God today and make with us an appeal to heaven that He might pour out His Spirit in unimaginable ways."[14]

Despite All of This . . .

Despite the many ways revival can be derailed, we should still continue praying for—and pressing in to—revival. One of the greatest hindrances to revival can actually be a cynical attitude toward the next move of God. Cynicism in the church stems from repeated disappointment in people and pastors who displayed various character flaws and left a trail of hurt and pain in their wake.

Brown says this happens when people see both the divine and the human side of revival. God can do something absolutely miraculous, but people can quickly muddy the waters. The pain of disappointment and division, he explains, can leave a bad taste in our mouths and provoke mixed feelings about another revival. If you are cynical and guarded, ask the Holy Spirit to heal your heart and renew your vision.

"Is our cynical attitude helping us to advance in the Lord?" Brown asks. "Is it helping us to grow in faith and fervor and passion and purity? Is it bringing joy and vitality to our hearts? Is it causing us to be more effective witnesses and more powerful warriors? Certainly not! Cynicism is not a fruit of the Spirit.

"It is true that people will fail, even in times of revival, but to let human failure rob us of the reality of revival is to give Satan a victory. It is time for us to arise out of the ashes of self-pity—or out of the pit of despair or out of the cozy cocoon of criticism, whatever our negative state may be—and it is time for us to put our hope afresh in the one true God. It is time to seek His face for revival again in this hour."[15]

Chapter 10

SUSTAINING REVIVAL UNTO REFORMATION

There is some talk in revival circles about sustainability—but wisdom dictates that revival can't ultimately be sustained long-term. Think about it for a minute. Although we can see a revival lifestyle, a church revival is typically marked by what I call marathon meetings. When revival hits a church or a territory, worship services are usually scheduled three, four, five times a week—or more.

Over the long haul that's not sustainable without burning out passionate believers with servants' hearts who ultimately still need to get up and go to work day in and day out. Revival shouldn't lead to burnout, but history shows that it has. Some have even blamed moral failures on the stress and strain of keeping a revival going. It was never God's plan to sustain the type of revival that is contained in the four walls of the church. Rather, revival should awaken society and drive transformation of a people and their community.

All that said, revival rarely dies in our hearts. Indeed, past revivals have certainly produced sustained spiritual fruit in our day. The Brownsville Revival, also known as the Pensacola Outpouring, began in 1995 and was marked by a call to holiness. More than four million people attended meetings over a five-year period, and many are still praying for the next revival. The Toronto Blessing, which started after pastors John and Carol Arnott visited revivals in Argentina and South Africa, sparked revivals in Atlanta, St. Louis, Anaheim, and as far as Albania and Cambodia.[1]

Many who were at the meetings in Brownsville and Toronto are now missionaries in various parts of the world, pastoring strong churches, operating Bible schools, and doing other mighty exploits for God's kingdom. These events in modern Christian history prove that it's possible for a revival to impact a generation of believers and spill over into the next generation.

Yet neither of these revivals or others that have emerged in the twentieth or twenty-first century have sparked a true great awakening. Could it be possible that revival didn't transition into awakening and transformation because revival waned in the hearts of the people? Or did we fall into one of the pitfalls we discussed in the previous chapter? Either way, what can we do about it? How can we realize transforming revival?

Progressing From Revival to Awakening

There is no standard recipe for awakening, but there are principles, including prayer, fasting, and repentance, that can prepare hearts for a visitation from the Lord. Clay Nash, senior leader at The CityGate in Southaven, Mississippi, outlines four elements necessary to see revival meetings progress into a sustained movement that triggers an awakening.

"All movements that have brought about significant change burst from hearts of conviction," Nash says. "Many believed that what God was doing in their midst was the genuine handiwork of God. Believing is awesome, but if your belief is not centered in conviction, then your belief will eventually turn into preference and you won't be willing to pay the price to sustain momentum that triggers awakening."[2]

Nash explains the important distinction between a belief and conviction this way: A belief is something we hold, such as a belief in the healing power of God or in the prophetic ministry. However, a conviction is something that holds us. Conviction, Nash says, is one of the many ways that God speaks to us and allows faith to come to us.

"Conviction will always drive us past the place of preference and convenience," Nash says. "If out of preference we pay tithe, study God's Word, or serve God's people, then eventually we will become indifferent toward the cost of breakthrough and prefer not to do any of the above. However, when God convicts us to do something, we don't see the greatness of the cost but the vastness of the reward. Conviction will always birth sacrifice, whereas preference will always look for the avenue of least resistance."[3]

Second, Nash says relational covenants must be established. Many revival meetings quickly wane—and lose their effectiveness—due to the emphasis on partnering for a series of revival meetings rather than coming together in an ongoing labor of love. "When God's Word speaks of where two or more come together agreeing as touching something, He is speaking of hearts touching in relational agreement—not just a covenant agreement of words," Nash says. "Out of covenant you can attain right standing before God, but only out of intimacy can you attain right relationship with God, which is truly what righteousness is. Relationship will hold people together when the covenant agreement becomes blurred or the covenant needs changing and adjusting."[4]

The third element is courage. Think about the great courage it takes to truly allow the Holy Spirit to be the Lord of the meetings. Nash says courage is a strength to say, day by day, "Lord, not my will but Your will be done." And he says courage is only found in hearts totally surrendered to God's will.

"It takes courage to embrace the grace of the unknown facts of what lies ahead," Nash says. "Only with a heart of courage can you see and embrace the circumstances at hand when the tide rolls in and brings with it debris from the bottom of the ocean that [aren't] pretty or easy to deal with."[5]

Finally, flexibility is vital to sustain a revival until it becomes an awakening. Nash says there must be a "constant endeavor" to remain fluid and flexible in order to remain effective in creating the momentum to move from revival into awakening. Then once you transition into awakening, there's another challenge: sustaining the awakening.

Six Keys to Sustaining Awakening

Larry Sparks, author of the books *Breakthrough Faith* and *Breakthrough Healing* and host of the weekly radio program *Voice of Destiny*, is a student of revivals—both modern and historical. He offers six keys for sustaining revival.

1. Recognize that revival is not personality driven but God focused.

He points to the Toronto Blessing as a good example of this, as the revival was never focused on Randy Clark or the Arnotts. "It was not about any of the speakers who preached from their pulpit," Sparks says. "It was about a radical, corporate hunger for God that transformed a little warehouse church in Canada to a center for historic out-pouring. Are we hungry for God? Not breakthrough. Not blessing. Not keys to improving our lives. Not even mani-festations of revival. How much do we simply want to know and experience God and see Jesus receive all the glory?"[6]

2. Develop a culture of testimony.

We discussed this in an earlier chapter, where Dutch Sheets explained that the Hebrew word for "testimony" is not just to say again but also to do again. As Sparks sees it, when we recognize that as God "freely gives" to us, we are called to "freely give" to the world, we become catalysts to carry revival. We've been freely given our testimony—from salvation to healing experiences to deliverances to various victories and God encounters.

"Our testimony is what we offer the world," Sparks says. "As we talk about what God has done for us, our words release new options to the people listening. They may have never heard that God is a loving Father. They may have never known that Jesus still heals today. There is a good chance that they had not been introduced to the Savior whose blood made complete atonement for all of their sins! By sharing your testimony, you introduce new options to other people, and along with those options, faith is released."[7]

3. Practice true repentance.

Indeed, Sparks says revival dies without repentance and points to repentance as essential to seeing lasting fruit from a spiritual outpouring. As Sparks sees it, there are two dimensions to repentance. We must confront the chasm of our sin, which then will produce true godly sorrow as we recognize the level of disagreement between our lives and what God has made available. Unfortunately we see too little preaching on repentance and too much preaching on prosperity to ever see a great awakening.

"Sorrow over sin is not designed to produce depressed, condemned believers," says Sparks. "It awakens us to the chasm between what we are presently experiencing of God and what He has truly made available. The chasm causes us to confess and repent for our sins and pursue God with greater passion. As a result, we begin to experience the river of God. Signs, wonders, and miracles start to break out. Healing—physically and emotionally—flows in an intense measure. People are dramatically touched by the power of God."[8]

4. Recognize that it is possible for revival to continue beyond a time, season, or even a generation.

For those of you who still have difficulty embracing this concept, Sparks suggests asking yourself, "What definition of revival am I embracing?" He goes on to say: "If we are looking for something new to come down from heaven, then yes, it will be difficult to sustain such an experience. This is what had led so many to try to repeat what they experienced during a previous move of God. As a result, they attempt to manufacture this experience, only to end up operating in the flesh."[9]

5. Stop and respond to God's sovereign summons.

When revival comes, Sparks says, it is easy to get caught up in the exciting whirlwind of salvations, God's presence, healings, miracles, and signs and wonders. He says all of these things are glorious, but they can be downright destructive if we do not receive and respond to the "memo."

"Revival preaches a very clear message: this is what normal Christianity looks like. Adjust accordingly!" Sparks says.

"Are we listening? The longer we deny that revival reveals what normal should look like, the longer we will be satisfied with a wind or a refreshing when, in fact, God wants to revolutionize Christian life as we know it. It is time for us to raise the bar and start agreeing with God's vision."[10]

6. Revival must reorient us in order to produce reformation.

Sparks explains it this way: we are reoriented with Jesus's original picture of "normal church" so that we can reform our operations appropriately. The problem, he says, is some people want revival without the reformation because the occasional, sporadic visitation does not threaten the safe, predictable, comfortable rhythm of Christian life.

"Ideally, we want a move of God that we can fit nicely into our twenty-first-century church paradigms," Sparks says. "We want a touch without having to engage transformation. Truly, this is like putting a square peg in a round hole. This will always be impossible, as the structure will need to change in order to carry revival. We pray for the new wine but are unwilling to trade our old wineskins."[11]

If we want to truly experience revival that leads to reformation, Sparks encourages us to begin by praying:

> *Holy Spirit, come. I want to experience Your presence and power like never before. I don't want just a touch or a visitation or a season of revival; I want to live like Jesus said I could live. Open my eyes. Show me areas in my church, life, and family that need to be transformed so that I can experience everything Jesus said was available and possible. Amen.*[12]

Characteristics of "Awakening" Leadership

Of course, without strong, discerning leadership in place, personal hunger can take revival and awakening only so far. If we want to see true and lasting transformation, we need a leadership structure in place that can shepherd the movement in a way that promotes kingdom purpose rather than denominations, doctrines, or even demonstrations.

Indeed, if we want to see an awakening that confronts and changes culture, we need to consider leadership. We've talked about the pitfalls of revival as it relates to leadership in a previous chapter, but what does awakening leadership look like?

Don Lynch, founding apostle of FreedomHouse, an apostolic resource center in Jacksonville, Florida, notes that it generally takes thirty to forty years from the time revival first hits for the fuller influence and kingdom reset to crest into a greater awareness of God in the culture. During this time, he says, the original leaders of revival may suffer rejection and even have their integrity and legitimacy questioned.

"Revival will manifest in various types of mini-movements, some of which will fall upon error or overemphasis of one aspect of how they experienced God," Lynch says. "The institutionalized church will distance itself from the new in order to preserve and maintain its status quo. Yet, a remnant remains that has matured the original fire to an international level of leadership, a level at which it can influence and impact a nation."[13]

As Lynch sees it, the goal is to blend existing leaders transformed after experiencing God in new ways with emerging leaders who are experiencing God for the first time. Those whom God uses to birth the move of God must mature in leadership so they can champion "the word of the Lord" in the culture. "God wants everybody, but He never starts with everybody," Lynch says. "He starts with a remnant and remnants start with leaders. More specifically, He starts with remnant leaders. Remnant leaders function as forerunners."[14]

Lynch offers a clear warning in a revival culture: immediately reject leaders who assume that the "forerunner" strategy required them to increase. God wants revival to become awakening unto transformation, and that demands "I die to produce life" leadership. This kind of leader moves the moment into a movement and feeds the momentum of the movement with emerging leaders. These new leaders can do what the forerunner does—and even greater works. Lynch says the "I must increase" leadership model is among the pitfalls we've discussed in earlier chapters and breeds doctrinal idols and personality cults.

"Awakening cannot be controlled by man or any particular kingdom leader. It immediately requires regional leadership that no one personality can provide," Lynch says. "Awakening is the work of Holy Spirit upon and through the kingdom that raises the awareness of God and His purpose in the general population. While God uses the forerunner and remnant leaders to prepare the Lord a people, the moment the awakening arrives, the identity of that forerunning leadership must radically shift. They must decrease during the season of revival in order for the leadership dynamics of the new season to increase."[15]

Whenever revival leaders demand to increase instead of decrease, Lynch says, they may successfully expand revival but it will not ultimately gain the spiritual momentum that can sustain transformation. When awakening comes, he says, it will redefine the revival that produced it, and redefine the forerunners and remnant leaders who birthed it.

"It is not a leader's role in the awakening to repeat the process but to provide blueprint leadership to the awakening about how to continue the preparation and positioning of awakening leaders," Lynch says. "The leaders experienced the process so thoroughly, deeply, and personally so they could understand the process that others will experience. They may receive an outcome that took you fifteen years in just fifteen days! They become an expert in the strategy of leadership development so they can provide leadership in the new season."[16]

Lynch is convinced of this: unless the forerunner leaders obey completely, submit completely, and transform completely, they will not be available to identify the difference between "what not to do" and "what to do"—and the awakening may degenerate into a charismatic Woodstock instead of maturing into a reformation. Moreover, he says, the preparation and positioning of kingdom leaders—not anointing; manifestations; activations; visions and dreams; or demonstrations of power, miracles, signs, and wonders— is the measuring standard of revival growth and maturity.

"The manifestations of a revival should produce maturity in leaders so those mature leaders can have greater influence and impact in the season of awakening," Lynch says, "not so those manifestations can become a monument to a moment. God will punch a move of God in the belly when it starts becoming a destination instead of a distribution center. The manifestations only produce maturity when they are part of a fathering and discipling process that prepares and positions people to produce purpose."[17]

Dealing With Leaders and Making Disciples

In this hour God is dealing with leaders and preparing a people for a visitation. Alistair Petrie, executive director of Partnership Ministries, which combines prayer and research in order to prepare communities, cities, nations, and the marketplace for lasting revival, authentic transformation, and the release of kingdom culture, sees us on the edge of an awakening—but God is tackling the issue of leadership in a way he has never before witnessed.

Petrie received this revelation while traveling through Greece's Kolona Port in 2013. Security personnel conducted a random search, and, as he puts it, "the searcher unfortunately pulled my trousers right down to the floor. I was in my underwear, totally exposed to everybody. It was one of those moments where I asked, 'What is going on here, Lord?' You could feel the people staring at me, and it was really embarrassing."[18]

Two days later, Petrie says the Holy Spirit answered his question with a word that should put the fear of the Lord into church leadership. The Lord said: "What you went through is what I'm about to take My leadership through. I'm going to strip them of everything just as My Son was stripped of His clothing. I'm going to be stripping My leaders because the time is so close. I cannot afford to have My leaders hiding anything where their character goes ahead of their anointing. I have to rein them in."[19]

Petrie later understood that God is stripping leadership of their desire to be seen, their issues with sexual immorality, and anything else that hinders His plan. Since Petrie received that word, a number of high-profile leaders have been exposed for "moral failures." But it's not all about the leadership. Petrie also sees the Lord searching to and fro for four types of disciples in this hour—what he calls Issachar people, Esther people, Daniel people, and Joseph people. "There were twenty-two aircrafts on 9/11 with supposed terrorists, and mine was one of them," Petrie says. "The Lord said to me in the plane that, 'This is the end of the age of innocence. It's a wake-up call. What you're seeing in the physical realm is an expression of the spiritual realm. Don't cave in to the fear of man any longer, and don't you ever preach the same way.' There's been a shift. We feel God is calling His church to be the people of Issachar, to read the signs of the times, or we will not have a legitimate prophetic voice. [We must have] an authentic word of God."[20]

We're also called to be Esther people who are here for such times as this—to be that authentic voice of God. Petrie is convinced that God is about to release His power in holiness, and He won't allow unholiness to touch His holiness. We're also called to be Daniel people, he says, as God calls leaders, nations, governments, and businesses to come to the church and ask us to offer insight into world events.

"We've watched this ever since the ISIS/ISIL issue came out into the open and Putin was doing his thing, and there was the missing aircraft," Petrie says. "We see all these incidents globally that are capturing the hearts and minds and horrifying people. It's shaking-up time unlike anything I've ever seen before—and we've been studying this for over twenty to twenty-five years. We're watching how God is shaking the ecology, the economy, finances, morality, the area of politics, the issues of the church at such a level that leaders are coming to say, 'What's going on?' We have to be Daniel people who can explain to the leaders and society what God is saying without fear and without embarrassment but also without presumptuousness. The humility issue—the power of moving in the opposite spirit—is one of the most powerful tools for preparing a city and land for authentic transformational revival."[21]

Finally, we need to be Joseph people. Petrie says we are being called to build up goods that we can share in the coming days. We may see a spiritual famine, and he's sure we will see physical famine. From Petrie's perspective, the cities in which God is doing an authentic work right now are cities marked by desperation, humility, and holiness; cities in which people are crying out to God for His purposes until they capture the heartbeat of God—and He shows up.

"In North America we have had our own way of doing things," Petrie says. "We've done church our own way, yet in some of the other nations we work in the hunger is so significant. God is uncovering, not out of anger but out of love. He's preparing, He's equipping, and He's really opening up the eyes of our hearts to see what He wants us to see, not out of our learned behavior but out of our coming before with a sense of humility and holiness, asking the right questions and fighting the right battles."[22]

Preparing the Church for Outpouring

Preparing for the next outpouring—the next great awakening—means leaders need to equip the saints for the work of the ministry, model the walk of humility and holiness, and fight the right battles. Churches will need to evolve from programmatic-centered congregations to kingdom-government clusters where the true fivefold ministry is operating to raise up believers to preach the gospel and make disciples—then mature them into kingdom leaders whom God can use to reform families, workplaces, and entire communities.

Churches need to "reorder their structures, provisions, and people in ways that prepare and position them to function when awakening arrives," Lynch says. "They should reset their leadership dynamics so that their present levels of hundreds or thousands can accommodate tens or even hundreds of thousands. They must be prepared to influence and impact regionally... The leaders in the state must learn to function at an international level no matter the scope of their leadership or the location of their assignments."[23]

When awakening comes, Lynch is convinced the Holy Spirit will assign and position thousands in a "forerunner" region to travel to other regions to prepare them for awakening as it spreads. This is an apostolic-prophetic paradigm rather than traditional church model that gathers rather than sends out. An apostolic-prophetic ministry paradigm goes beyond the local church into the surrounding territory as the Holy Spirit wills.

Lynch points to Acts 19 as a model for the process and progress of a region first touched by a forerunner, then becoming a forerunner region, and then becoming an apostolic and prophetic epicenter that provides international-level leadership. Acts 19 also shows how these forerunners became fathering leaders through which Ephesus turned into the center of Christianity for two hundred years.

"Paul spent three years there preparing and positioning kingdom leaders," Lynch says. "He had revival and riot. The 'what is' didn't limit his function in producing the 'what is coming next.'... After resistance from 'what is,' Paul moved to an apostolic training center, prepared, and positioned leaders who could influence and impact the entire region...In a very short time, through an awakening, the kingdom ecclesia in the region exploded, influenced, and impacted the culture of Asia Minor."[24]

I believe it's going to happen again. God is inviting people to pray. If we continue to cry out to Him, we will see a visitation that will bring transforming revival. Leaders must begin to prepare now for the coming outpouring. Churches must be ready to bring in the harvest. We need to pray as if it depends on God and prepare as if it depends on us. That combination will set the stage to sustain an awakening like nothing the world has ever seen.

Chapter 11

REVIVAL BEGINS
WITH YOU

IF YOU ARE reading this book, you are probably among the remnant who yearn to see signs, wonders, and miracles manifest today as they did in the Book of Acts. The Acts of the Apostles never fails to fascinate my heart. It is the Holy Ghost in action, the gifts of the Spirit made manifest, a passionate believer's delight. Indeed, many of us want to see the Holy Spirit move in the church—and in the world—like that again. Well, I beseech you to consider these four words: *revival begins with you.*

We can see revival unto awakening unto reformation unto transformation. But we have to be willing to take a leap of faith as the early church did. We have to be willing to pay a price to walk as they walked. We have to be willing to pray without ceasing. We have to be willing to die daily as the apostle Paul committed to do. We have to be willing to relinquish control to the Holy Spirit so He can move as He wants to move. We have to be willing to repent for the character flaws that hold us back. We have to be willing to cooperate with the grace of God to yield to His work in our souls. We have to be willing to walk in love and unity with true believers whose views on nonessentials aren't exactly the same as ours. We have to be willing to war against the spirit of compromise that is raging against the church in this age. We just have to be willing. Revival begins with you—and me.

Despite 24/7 prayer movements that bear plenty of fruit, we don't see people waiting to stand in our shadows hoping to get healed. Despite the apostolic movement rising in this hour, we rarely see people raised from the dead. Despite large stadiums of sincere people repenting in tears before the Lord for the sins of generations, we are a far cry from the reality of the Book of Acts. Sure, we see a ration of revival spring up from time to time, and I believe the beginnings of awakening are emerging even now. We see a measure of the miraculous. We see demons cast out in the name of Jesus. But it still doesn't compare to the Book of Acts, does it? Revival—the Third Great Awakening—begins with you—and me.

We can't do the Lord's part—we can't force miracles, signs, and wonders. But we can do our part—we can tear down the strongholds in our own souls that are preventing us from walking in the fullness of the Spirit. We can stop tolerating worldly entertainment and fleshly lusts that tempt us to sin. We can start interceding for the fallen saints instead of playing judge. In other words, we can start living as the saints lived in the Book of Acts: sold out, on fire, and ready to die for the gospel. Revival begins with you—and me.

Again, we can't manufacture miracles. We can't work up wonders. But we can cooperate with the Holy Spirit to separate the profane from the holy in our own hearts and in our own minds. We can purge ourselves and lay aside every weight that holds us back. We can allow the Spirit of God to do a deep work *in* us so the Spirit of God can do a great work *through* us. Revival begins with you—and me.

Michael Brown, speaker, author, radio-show host, revivalist, and theologian, puts it this way: "If there is one thing I have learned…is that everything flows out of our personal relationship with the Lord, that the inner life is more essential than the outward life, that our private walk with God is more important than our public ministry for God, that personal revival takes precedence over corporate revival. After all, the Body of Christ is made up of individuals, and it will never be stronger as a unit than it is individually."[1]

Seven Signs You Need Personal Revival

A. W. Tozer, a pastor, author, magazine editor, and spiritual mentor to many, encouraged believers to consider seven points of self-discovery that speak to our spiritual health: (1) what we want most, (2) what we think about most, (3) how we use our money, (4) what we do with our leisure time, (5) the company we enjoy, (6) whom and what we admire, and (7) what we laugh at.[2] With that in mind, Daniel K. Norris, a revivalist who served with the late Steve Hill for more than a decade, offers seven signs that you need revival in your life.[3]

1. You are entertained by things that once grieved you.

"Are you turning on things that once you would have turned off?" Norris asks. "When is the last time you walked out of a movie because you were grieved over how they profaned the name of your God? Are peers comfortable sharing obscene jokes in your presence, or do they change their tone when you're around? Are you entertaining yourself with things that once grieved you?"

2. You are silent where you once spoke.

"The truest evidence of the baptism of the Holy Spirit is a tongue that has been set free and set on fire with the gospel," Norris says. "Remember when you were first saved? You wanted to share the experience with your friends and family. Remember that boldness to declare His righteousness and what He had done for you? Do you still have it, or has your voice grown still? Your silence may be the sign of a backslidden heart."

3. Your prayer closet has cobwebs and your Bible is dusty.

"No man is greater than his own prayer life," says Norris. "...When life throws a problem your way, is prayer the first place you turn or the last? What did God show you in His Word today? When is the last time you spent quality time with the Lord? If you were as lacking in your vocation as you are in your devotion, how long would it be until you were out of work? Do you believe prayer truly works? Then you should be praying more!"

4. You're more likely to criticize your pastor than to contemplate his message.

"When you walk out of church, are you thinking about what you agreed and disagreed with in the message, or do you take it to heart? Criticism is a sure symptom of a heart that is hardening," Norris says. "I've learned in my own life that when I am criticizing another person, it says more about me than it does about them. Why not attend church this weekend and ask the Lord to speak to your heart and change your life through the words spoken from your pastor?"

5. You excuse sin.

"Sin is anything Jesus wouldn't do. I like this simple and straightforward definition. If Jesus wouldn't go there, do that, drink that, smoke that, say that, listen to that or watch that, then it is sin and has no place in the life [of] a son or daughter of God," Norris says. "…Are you tolerating habits and addictions? What are the hidden things in your life you wouldn't want anyone else to find out about? What do you keep telling yourself—'It's no big deal'? If you have sin in your life, don't excuse it. Confess it!"

6. You don't like to be confronted with truth.

"If I'm sick, I want a doctor to diagnose the problem, not tell me how great I am," Norris says. "If I'm unhealthy, I want a good friend to care enough to confront me about my eating habits. If I'm swimming in a mountain of debt, I don't need a friend offering me another loan; I need a true friend to cut up my credit cards."

7. You have a deep sense there's something more.

Says Norris: "Edwards and Wesley awakened our nation. Charles Finney was baptized in waves and waves of liquid love. William Seymour lived in the glory cloud for four years at Azusa. Smith Wigglesworth raised the dead back to life. I am jealous of their God encounters and will not be denied my own!"

Four Keys to Personal Revival

If Norris's words stirred your heart, you are not alone. There's a divine discontent coming back to the body of Christ. There are cries for revival that are reaching God's ears. But where do we go from here? How do we enter into personal revival that sets the stage for corporate revival?

Norris went on to offer four keys to revival—four principles that are worth putting into practice: a humble heart, persistent prayer, holy hunger, and radical repentance. Let's look briefly at each.[4]

1. A humble heart

"True humility is found when we come to the end of ourselves," Norris says. "This is the poverty of the spirit that Jesus said opens up the kingdom of God in Matthew 5:3. If we want revival, we have to humble ourselves and understand that there is nothing that we have or can do within our 'self' that has any value. True humility is returning to the Lord as our only hope and source. It means absolute dependence upon God."

2. Persistent prayer

"A saint who can kneel in prayer will never struggle to stand in public," says Norris. "…Revival comes in answer to the effective, fervent prayers of faith-filled men and women. This means revival is not found in a place, but a position. That position is on our knees in prayer. If you want to see revival birthed in your nation, church, or family, let it first be birthed in you. Go to God in prayer and don't stop until revival has touched your spirit."

3. Holy hunger

"Jesus said those who hunger and thirst for righteousness shall be filled. Are you still hungry? Do you still thirst for more of Him?" Norris asks. "If so, it's time to abandon every other pursuit and concentrate on chasing after the one thing that truly matters."

4. Radical repentance

"Without repentance, revival is impossible! This damnable doctrine from hell that would cheapen grace and remove the wonder of repentance keeps true revival from ever touching our land," says Norris. "Repentance is not a work of the flesh; it is a work of grace. By His grace we are convicted of unrighteousness and by His grace we are enabled to repent. I am so thankful that those whom the Lord loves He chastens!"

Pursuing His Presence

Of course, there is no recipe for revival. It's a matter of desperation. It's a matter of pursuit. It's a matter of refusing to stop pressing in to Him despite the circumstances raging against your life. It's about endeavoring to know Him and the power of His resurrection and being willing to share in His sufferings, even becoming like Him in His death, as Paul wrote to the church at Philippi (Phil. 3:10).

"Presence always wins out over principles," says Bill Johnson, senior pastor of Bethel Church in Redding, California, and author of *Face to Face With God: The Ultimate Quest to Experience His Presence*. "When we encounter His divine presence, transformation occurs that goes beyond the reach of merely good ideas—this is the transformation that first takes place within us that we might cause transformation around us. The heart to seek God is birthed in us by God Himself. Like all desires, it is not something that can be legislated or forced, but rather it grows within us as we become exposed to God's nature."[5]

In *Face to Face With God* Johnson collected the words of revivalists and healing evangelists of days gone by who successfully sought God's presence. I want to share some of their longings and prayers with you to illustrate the kind of passion for God's presence that leads to revival.

Evan Roberts's God encounter

Evan Roberts was the principle figure in the Welsh Revival of 1904–1905. It was the largest Christian revival in Wales in the twentieth century and sent waves of revival to other nations. W. T. Stead, author of the 1905 book *The Story of the Welsh Revival*, records Roberts as saying this:

> For a long, long time, I was much troubled in my soul and my heart by thinking over the failure of Christianity…but that night, after I had been in great distress praying about this, I went to sleep, and at 1 am in the morning suddenly I was wakened up…and found myself with unspeakable joy and awe in the very presence of the Almighty God. And for the space of four hours I was privileged to speak face to face with Him, as a man speaks with a friend. At 5 am it seemed to me as if I again returned to earth…And it was not only that morning, but every morning for three or four months…I felt it and it seemed to change all my nature, and I saw things in a different light, and I knew that God was going to work in the land, and not in this land only but in all the world.[6]

John G. Lake's yearning

John G. Lake was a businessman-turned-missionary and is best remembered as a faith healer. Lake founded the Apostolic Faith Mission of South Africa after he received the baptism of the Holy Spirit during the Azusa Street Revival in 1907. Greatly influenced by the healing ministry of John Alexander Dowie, Lake launched "healing rooms" in Spokane, Washington. His "Divine Healing Technicians," as they were called, reported more than one hundred thousand healings. The healing rooms movement continues to this day, with thousands of healing rooms around the world.

Lake expressed his hunger for God this way:

> My soul was crying out to God in a yearning too deep for words, when suddenly it seemed to me, that I had passed under a shower of warm tropical rain, which was not falling upon me, but through me. My spirit, and soul and body under this influence soothed into such a deep still calm, as I had never known. My brain, which had always been so active, became perfectly still. An awe of the presence of God settled over me. I knew it was God.
>
> Some moments passed; I do not know how many. The Spirit said, "I have heard your prayers, I have seen your tears. You are now Baptized in the Holy Spirit." Then currents of power began to rush through my being from the crown of my head to the soles of my feet. The shocks of power increased in rapidity, and voltage. As these currents of power would pass through me, they seemed to come upon my head, rush through my body, and through my feet into the floor.[7]

Charles Finney's overwhelming encounter

Charles Finney was a leader in the Second Great Awakening and is often considered the father of modern revivalism. He was certainly a reformer, leading the abolition of slavery and pushing for equal education for women and African Americans. He's remembered for his innovative preaching, allowing women to pray in public, and holding meetings with both men and women in the congregation.

He started the "anxious bench" so people considering accepting Christ could sit and receive prayer. He also called out sinners by name in his sermons and prayers. Bold.[8]

Let's listen in on one of his personal encounters with the presence of God.

> Just before evening the thought took possession of my mind, that as soon as I was left alone in the new office, I would try to pray again—that I was not going to abandon the subject of religion and give it up, at any rate; and therefore, although I no longer had any concern about my soul, still I would continue to pray.
>
> By evening we got the books and furniture adjusted; and I made up, in an open fire-place, a good fire, hoping to spend the evening alone. Just at dark Squire W—, seeing that everything was adjusted, bade me good-night and went to his home. I had accompanied him to the door; and as I closed the door and turned around, my heart seemed to be liquid within me. All my feelings seemed to rise and flow out; and the utterance of my heart was, "I want to pour my whole soul out to God." The rising of my soul was so great that I rushed into the room behind the front office to pray.
>
> There was no fire, and no light, in the room; nevertheless it appeared to me as if it were perfectly light. As I went in and shut the door after me, it seemed as if I met the Lord Jesus Christ face to face. It did not occur to me then, nor did it for some time afterward, that it was wholly a mental state. On the contrary, it seemed to me that I saw Him as I would see any other man. He said nothing, but looked at me in such a manner as to break me right down at His feet. I have always since regarded this as a most remarkable state

of mind; for it seemed to me a reality, that He stood before me, and I fell down at His feet and poured out my soul to Him. I wept aloud like a child, and made such confessions as I could with my choked utterance. It seemed to me that I bathed His feet with my tears; and yet I had no distinct impression that I touched Him, that I recollect.

I must have continued in this state for a good while; but my mind was too much absorbed with the interview to recollect anything that I said. But I know, as soon as my mind became calm, I returned to the front office, and found that the fire that I had made of large wood was nearly burned out. But as I turned and was about to take a seat by the fire, I received a mighty baptism of the Holy Ghost. Without any expectation of it, without ever having the thought in my mind that there was any such thing for me, without any recollection that I had ever heard the thing mentioned by any person in the world, the Holy Spirit descended upon me in a manner that seemed to go through me, body and soul. I could feel the impression, like a wave of electricity, going through and through me. Indeed it seemed to come in waves and waves of liquid love; for I could not express it in any other way. It seemed like the very breath of God. I can recollect distinctly that it seemed to fan me, like immense wings.

No words can express the wonderful love that was shed abroad in my heart. I wept aloud with joy and love; and I do not know but I should say, I literally bellowed out the unutterable gushings of my heart. These waves came over me, and over me, and over me, one after the other, until I recollect I cried out, "I shall die if these waves continue to pass over me."

I said, "Lord, I cannot bear any more;" yet I had no fear of death.[9]

Smith Wigglesworth meets the Spirit of God

Known as the "apostle of faith," Smith Wigglesworth was a pioneer of the Pentecostal revival at the turn of the twentieth century. Born to a poor family, the British plumber gave his heart to the Lord later in life, but he had a faith healing ministry that saw several people raised from the dead, along with blind eyes opened, deaf ears healed, and the paralyzed walk.

Wigglesworth also had a dramatic experience with the Holy Spirit.

> For four days I wanted nothing but God. But after that, I felt I should leave for my home, and I went to the Episcopal vicarage to say good-bye. I said to Mrs. Boddy, the vicar's wife: "I am going away, but I have not received the tongues yet." She answered, "It is not tongues you need, but the Baptism." "I have received the Baptism, Sister," I protested, "but I would like to have you lay hands on me before I leave." She laid her hands on me and then had to go out of the room. The fire fell. It was a wonderful time as I was there with God alone. He bathed me in power. I was conscious of the cleansing of the precious Blood, and I cried out: "Clean! Clean! Clean!" I was filled with the joy of the consciousness of the cleansing. I was given a vision in which I saw the Lord Jesus Christ. I beheld the empty Cross, and I saw Him exalted at the right hand of God the Father. I could speak no longer in English but I began to praise Him in other tongues as the Spirit of God gave me utterance. I knew then, although I might have received anointings previously,

that now, at last I had received the real baptism in the Holy Spirit as they received on the day of Pentecost.[10]

Where Do We Go From Here?

Ryan LeStrange is the leader of Impact International Ministries, a network of churches and ministries around the world with a single vision: to birth revival. He hosts a weekly prophetic television show on GOD TV called *Power4Today* and sees God birthing a desire in ministry leaders to abandon the normal way of doing things and press in to experience the fire of revival.

"This will mean a shift in the thinking and attitudes of the people who are part of these ministries. No longer can we be content just to have services void of the presence of God. Our heart's cry must be that God would come and fill the church with His manifest presence, glory, and power!" says LeStrange, author of *The Fire of Revival*. "God wants to come and occupy every place of worship with His majestic power. This is an hour of the supernatural. We will encounter angels, see visions, and dream dreams on an unprecedented level. God has planned an almighty outpouring in the final age to awaken the church and shake the nations."[11]

Mike Bickle, director of the International House of Prayer in Kansas City, says it like this: "No one can come face-to-face with what God is like and ever be the same."[12] That, he explains, is because His personality touches the depths of our emotions, which leads us to spiritual wholeness and maturity.

"Beholding the glory of who He is and what He has done renews our minds, strengthens us, and transforms us," Bickle says. "...I believe the greatest problem in the church is that we have an entirely inadequate and distorted idea of God's heart. We can experience short-term renewal through prayer and ministry. But to achieve long-term renewal and freedom, we must change our ideas about who God is."[13]

What does Bickle mean by this? Ask yourself these questions: In your most private thoughts, what do you believe God's personality is like? How does God feel about you when you stumble in sin and cry out to Him with a broken heart? How are you in God? How much intimacy do you really want with God? How passionate for Jesus do you want to be? How badly do you want to see personal revival that spills over into corporate revival, awakening, reformation, and transformation?

"The promise of being transformed and ignited to holy passion by understanding God's glorious personality is for everyone," assures Bickle. "No matter how weak or strong we feel, regardless of our previous failures, irrespective of our natural temperaments and personalities, each one of us can be ablaze with passion for Jesus...Passion for Jesus comes first and foremost by seeing His passion for us. Through frustration, condemnation, and heartache, I came to realize what ignites a heart with passion. The same can happen for you. It can happen to anyone who wants to experience passion for Jesus."[14]

Chapter 12

MAKING AN APPEAL
TO HEAVEN

IN THE SEVENTEENTH century, Bible commentator Matthew Henry wrote, "When God intends great mercy for His people, He first sets them praying."[1] God has set His people praying in America—and in many nations of the earth. Not only is the prayer movement gaining momentum with houses of day-and-night prayer rising around the world, but also I believe we're seeing the biggest reset of the prayer movement in decades.

Jack Hayford, founding pastor of The Church On The Way in Van Nuys, California, and former president of the International Church of the Foursquare Gospel, says he feels an urgency that we are at a point where desperate action is needed. As he sees it, for another great awakening to occur, the church and believers must engage in "gut-level, spiritually impassioned intercessory prayer."[2]

"The undermining of the ensconced dark powers that are eating out the underpinnings of our national life are only going to be neutralized and cast down in one way," says Hayford, author of *Penetrating the Darkness: Discovering the Power of the Cross Against Unseen Evil.* "You can preach about it, and that's valid, and it's not worthless. But it's what is awakened in the church through prayer that becomes the truly penetrating and ultimately victorious dynamic."[3]

It's time to make an appeal to heaven.

Agreeing With the Prayers of American Pioneers

Many are responding to the call. I believe one strategy for this appeal to heaven is tapping into the synergy of the ages, as Dutch Sheets explained it in an earlier chapter—to agree with the prayers of our Founding Fathers. By agreeing with the prayers, I mean to either pray the same prayer or to agree with the substance of the prayer as you make intercession for the nation. Here's a powerful prayer from President George Washington as part of his Thanksgiving Proclamation penned on October 3, 1789:

> Whereas it is the duty of all Nations to acknowledge the providence of Almighty God, to obey his will, to be grateful for his benefits, and humbly to implore his protection and favor-- and whereas both Houses of Congress have by their joint Committee requested me to recommend to the People of the United States a day of public thanksgiving and prayer to be observed by acknowledging with grateful hearts the many signal favors of Almighty God especially by affording them an opportunity peaceably to establish a form of government for their safety and happiness.
>
> Now therefore I do recommend and assign Thursday the 26th day of November next to be devoted by the People of these States to the service of that great and glorious Being, who is the beneficent Author of all the good that was, that is, or that will be-- That we may then all unite in rendering unto

him our sincere and humble thanks--for his kind care and protection of the People of this Country previous to their becoming a Nation--for the signal and manifold mercies, and the favorable interpositions of his Providence which we experienced in the course and conclusion of the late war--for the great degree of tranquility, union, and plenty, which we have since enjoyed--for the peaceable and rational manner, in which we have been enabled to establish constitutions of government for our safety and happiness, and particularly the national One now lately instituted--for the civil and religious liberty with which we are blessed; and the means we have of acquiring and diffusing useful knowledge; and in general for all the great and various favors which he hath been pleased to confer upon us.

and also that we may then unite in most humbly offering our prayers and supplications to the great Lord and Ruler of Nations and beseech him to pardon our national and other transgressions-- to enable us all, whether in public or private stations, to perform our several and relative duties properly and punctually--to render our national government a blessing to all the people, by constantly being a Government of wise, just, and constitutional laws, discreetly and faithfully executed and obeyed--to protect and guide all Sovereigns and Nations (especially such as have shewn kindness unto us) and to bless them with good government, peace, and concord--To promote the knowledge and practice of true religion and virtue, and the encrease of science among them and us--and generally to grant unto all Mankind such a degree of temporal prosperity as he alone knows to be best.[4]

Prayers of the American Presidents, compiled by Larry Keefauver, offers an in-depth study of the prayers of our nation's presidents throughout history, including pioneers of awakening such as John Adams, Thomas Jefferson, James Madison, and John Quincy Adams. It also offers insights into how Abraham Lincoln, Franklin Roosevelt, John F. Kennedy, and George W. Bush—presidents who served during times of crisis—prayed for the nation. Again, we can come into agreement with the prayers of past presidents—and we need to in this hour—by reading them and simply declaring that "I agree with the prayers of George Washington over America.

Agreeing With the Prayers of Revivalists

Revivalists through the ages have lifted up many heartfelt cries to the Lord. Most that I find recorded in history are personal prayers that would strengthen the ministers to carry forth the Lord's will. Considering that revival starts with you—and me—and considering that we cannot see community transformation without personal transformation, these personal prayers are pivotal.

Reuben "Uncle Bud" Robinson was born in a simple log cabin in the Tennessee mountains. He came to know the Lord in 1880 during a camp meeting, and he sensed a call to preach. He had no education and stuttered badly, but he prayed, "O Lord, give me a backbone as big as a saw log, and ribs like sleepers under the church floor. Put iron shoes on me and galvanized breeches, and hang a wagonload of determination in the gable end of my soul. And help me to sign the contract to fight the devil as long as I have vision, and bite him as long as I have a tooth, and then gum him till I die! Amen!"[5] Robinson traveled about two million miles during his ministry, preached more than thirty-three thousand sermons, saw more than one hundred thousand conversions, and much more. Prayer works!

Thomas á Kempis, a fifteenth-century German canon and the author of *The Imitation of Christ*, offered many prayers in his book that we would do well to pray daily. He offers the prayer for the spirit of devotion, the prayer to be enabled to do God's will perfectly, a prayer against evil thoughts, a prayer for the enlightenment of the mind, and a prayer for cleansing of the heart and for heavenly wisdom. Let's pray that last prayer now:

> Strengthen me, O God, by the grace of Thy Holy Spirit. Give me virtue to be strengthened with might in the inner man, and to free my heart from all fruitless care and trouble, and that I be not drawn away by various desires after any things whatsoever, whether of little value or great, but that I may look upon all as passing away, and myself as passing away with them; because there is no profit under the sun, and all is vanity and vexation of spirit. [Ecclesiastes ii. 11] Oh how wise is he that considereth thus!
>
> Give me, O Lord, heavenly wisdom, that I may learn to seek Thee above all things and to find Thee; to relish Thee above all things and to love Thee; and to understand all other things, even as they are, according to the order of Thy wisdom. Grant me prudently to avoid the flatterer, and patiently to bear with him that opposeth me; for this is great wisdom, not to be carried by every wind of words, nor to give ear to the wicked flattering Siren; for thus do we go safely on in the way we have begun.[6]

Jonathan Edwards, a key figure in the First Great Awakening and the man who preached the sermon "Sinners in the Hands of an Angry God" that people are still talking about today, was on guard against the spirit of pride. In his work *Thoughts on Revival and Religion in New England, A.D. 1740*, he asks for prayers from his readers:

> If I have assumed too much in the following discourse, and have spoken in a manner that savors of a spirit of pride, no wonder that others can better discern it than I myself. If it be so, I ask pardon, and beg the prayers of every Christian reader that I may have more light, humility and zeal; and that I may be favored with such measures of the divine Spirit as a minister of the Gospel stands in need of at such an extraordinary season.[7]

We don't know everything the revivalists from days gone by prayed for, but we do know that they prayed for revival. Charles H. Spurgeon, known as the "prince of preachers" and a key figure in the Second Great Awakening, said this: "Oh! men and brethren, what would this heart feel if I could but believe that there were some among you who would go home and pray for a revival of religion—men whose faith is large enough, and their love fiery enough to lead them from this moment to exercise unceasing intercessions that God would appear among us and do wondrous things here, as in the times of former generations."[8]

Biblical Prayers for Modern-Day Revivalists

The Bible is full of scriptures we can use as a basis of our prayers for revival and awakening in our land. Here are a few worth meditating on and releasing back to God. It all begins with building your faith in the everlasting God, who hears our prayers and delivers us from evil. Psalm 77, which is too long to include in its entirety here, is a good place to start encouraging your heart by remembering God's redemptive works. You can read these prayers quietly and let your heart agree with the words, or you can read them and call those things that are not as though they were. (See Romans 4:17.)

From there we need to express our awareness that our nation has strayed from God. Although the problems in our nation began many decades ago, we must, like Daniel, stand in the gap and repent for the sins of generations past and our own sins. Ezra 9:6–8 is a powerful model prayer you can adapt for the state of our nation. You can pray this aloud in your prayer closet or have one person read it aloud in a corporate prayer meeting as intercessors agree in their hearts:

> O my God, I am ashamed and embarrassed to lift up my face to You, my God, because our iniquities have expanded over our heads and our wrongdoing has grown up to the heavens. Since the days of our fathers until this day, we have been in a great guilt. It is because of our iniquities that we, our kings, and our priests have been delivered—by the sword, by captivity, by spoil, and by being shamed—into the hand of the kings of the lands. This day is like that, too.
>
> Yet now for a little while, there has been a favorable response from the LORD our God—leaving us a remnant to escape, giving us a tent peg from His holy place, having our eyes enlightened by our God, and giving us a little reviving in our bondage.

What we need is God's mercy. Thankfully He is rich in mercy and slow to anger (Ps. 86:15). I believe God's hand of discipline is upon our nation even now, and if we don't repent and cry out for mercy, we will see a heavier hand. God's motive in judgment is love. He is trying to save us from ourselves. You can find plenty of verses in Psalms to this end and turn them into prayers.

Here are a few:

> Restore us again, O LORD God of Hosts;
>   cause Your face to shine,
>   and we shall be delivered.
>
> —PSALM 80:19

> Restore us, O God of our salvation,
>   and put away Your indignation toward us.
> Will You be angry with us forever?
>   Will You draw out Your anger to all generations?
> Will You not revive us again,
>   that Your people may rejoice in You?
> Show us Your mercy, O LORD,
>   and grant us Your deliverance.
>
> —PSALM 85:4–7

> Remember this, that the enemy has scorned, O
>   LORD,
>   and that the foolish people have blasphemed Your
>   name.
> Do not give the life of Your turtledove to a wild
>   animal;
>   do not forget the life of Your poor forever.
>   Have regard for the covenant; for the dark
>   places of the earth are full of the habitations of
>   violence.
> May the oppressed not return ashamed;
>   may the poor and needy praise Your name.

Arise, O God, plead Your own cause;
    remember how the fool insults You daily.
Do not forget the voice of Your enemies,
    the tumult of those who rise up against You
      continually.
                    —PSALM 74:18–23

We need God's power to break into the situation in our nation. We can't turn this around without His divine intervention. We need Him to show up on the scene and awaken hearts with His presence. We need an outpouring of the gifts of the Spirit—signs, wonders, and miracles—that demand the attention of even the hardest hearts.

We can pray along these lines:

Oh, that You would rend the heavens and come
    down,
    that the mountains might shake at Your presence,
as when the melting fire burns,
    as the fire causes the waters to boil,
to make Your name known to Your adversaries,
    that the nations may tremble at Your presence!
When You did awesome things for which we did not
    look,
    You came down; the mountains quaked at Your
      presence.
For since the beginning of the world men have not
    heard,
    nor perceived by ear,
neither has the eye seen a God besides You,
    who acts for the one who waits for Him.
                    —ISAIAH 64:1–4

Agreeing With Today's Prayer Warriors

Of course, making intercession unto a Third Great Awakening isn't just about agreeing with the prayers of the Founding Fathers, the historic revivalists, or even the "great cloud of witnesses" who left record of prayers of repentance and for revival in the Scriptures. Modern-day apostles, prophets, evangelists, pastors, and teachers are praying fervently for revival in America. I want to share three prayers from modern-day intercessors that I encourage you to come into agreement with.

Kenneth Copeland, an internationally known speaker, author, television minister, and recording artist, offers this prayer for revival:

> Lord, start revival in me first. I am Your servant and I place myself in position to receive revival. I feed on the Scriptures as a sheep feeds in green pastures because Your words are life to me. Holy Spirit of God, You raised Jesus from the dead and You dwell in me. So, I yield to You to energize my spirit, restore my soul and rejuvenate my mortal body. I renew my mind with Your Word. In my innermost being is a well of living water and I am revived!
>
> Revival not only is life to me, but life to everyone who calls on the Name of the LORD. Therefore, I intercede on behalf of the people. I call upon You as the God of Abraham, Isaac and Jacob. I call upon the mighty Name of Jesus. All of mankind needs life, Lord! All of mankind needs revival because it is life— Your life. I speak and sow seeds of revival everywhere I go. I send forth angels to reap the harvest of revival all over the world. I put my hand to the sickle to reap the rich harvest of revival in my home, my church,

my community, in the marketplace, on the job, in my country and in all the world. Pour Yourself out on the people. Lord of the harvest, send forth laborers, positioning them in strategic places to minister as You pour out Your Spirit on all flesh. Almighty God, show Yourself mighty and strong with signs and wonders. Holy Spirit, breathe on all the people of the world. I pray this in the Name above all names, Jesus. Amen.[9]

Anne Graham Lotz, the daughter of evangelist Billy Graham, released this powerful prayer on the National Day of Prayer in 2014:

Lord of the Universe. Lord of this planet. Lord of the nations. Lord of our hearts. On this National Day of Prayer, we look to You…

In the darkness, You are our Light.

In the storm, You are our Anchor.

In our weakness, You are our Strength. In our grief, You are our Comfort.

In our despair, You are our Hope.

In our confusion, You are our Wisdom. In time of terrorism, You are our Shield. In time of war, You are our Peace.

In times of uncertainty, You are the Rock on which we stand.

We make our prayer to You using the words of the prophet Daniel:

O Lord, You are the great and awesome God, who keeps His covenant of love with those who love Him and keep His commandments. You are merciful and forgiving. You are righteous, but this day we are covered with shame because we have sinned against You, and done wrong. We have turned away from Your commands and principles. We have turned away from You.

Yet You have promised in 2 Chronicles 7, that if we—a people identified with You—would humble ourselves, pray, seek Your face, and turn from our wicked ways, then You would hear our prayer, forgive our sin and heal our land.

So we choose to stop pointing our finger at the sins of others, and examine our own hearts and lives. We choose to acknowledge our own sin—our neglect and defiance and ignorance and even rejection of You. This day we choose to repent.

In response to our heartfelt repentance, God of Abraham, Isaac and Jacob, Father of Jesus Christ, in keeping with all Your righteous acts and according to Your promise, turn away Your anger and Your wrath from the United States of America. Hear the prayers and petitions offered to You on this National Day of Prayer, as we give You our full attention. Give ear, our God, and hear; open Your eyes and see. We do not make requests of You because we are righteous, but because of Your great mercy.

For the glory of Your Name hear our prayer, forgive our sin, and heal our land.

We ask this in the name of Your Son Jesus Christ who offers us salvation from Your judgment, forgiveness for our sin, and reconciliation with You through His own blood shed on the Cross. Amen.[10]

Greg Laurie, evangelist and senior pastor of Harvest Christian Fellowship in Riverside, California, offered this petition on the National Day of Prayer in 2013:

Father, we come to You to pray for our nation, the United States of America.

How You have blessed us through the years, Lord! We rightly sing, "America, America, God shed His grace on thee." Yet we see trouble in our culture today. We see the breakdown of the family, crippling addictions, and random acts of horrific violence.

Lord, we need Your help in America. In recent days, we have done our best to remove Your Word and Your counsel from our courtrooms, classrooms and culture. It seems, as President Lincoln once said, that we have "forgotten God." But Lord, You have not forgotten us! You can bless and help and revive our country again.

Scripture tells us that "Righteousness exalts a nation, but sin is a reproach to any people" (Proverbs 14:34). Lord, in Your mercy, we ask that You would exalt our country again. We have had a number of great awakenings in America. We have experienced times of refreshing, and revivals that changed not only the spiritual but also the moral landscape. As the psalmist said, "Will You not revive us again, so that Your people may rejoice in You?" (Psalm 85:6)

That is our prayer for America today, Lord. Send a mighty spiritual awakening that will turn the hearts of men and women, boys and girls back to you. You have told us if we will humble ourselves and pray, and seek Your face and turn from our wicked ways, that You will forgive our sins and heal our land. (2 Chronicles 7:14)

Forgive us today, Lord, and heal this troubled land that we love so much.

We ask all of this in the name of Jesus Christ, Amen![11]

We Must Do More Than Pray

Prayer is the foundation for everything we do—but prayer is not the place to stop. Prayer is the jumping-off point. Prayer is the place where we hear from God so we can take faith-based action. Faith without works is dead, and prayer is not an end to itself. Although I believe there's been a lot more action than prayer in recent years, we can't stop taking action. It's not an either-or proposition—it's a both-and agenda.

Cindy Jacobs, cofounder of Generals International, launched the United States Reformation Prayer Network (USRPN) in part to link prayer with activism. She asked a question to the USRPN leaders—and it's a question you may have asked yourself after so many decades of prayer without societal transformation. Jacobs's question was this: We have prayed for the ending of abortion and for the United States to be a righteous nation; why haven't we succeeded?

> Here is Jacobs's response: The cumulative answer was that we needed not only to pray, but we needed to act. We now call the marriage of these two, prayer activism. What does this mean? We need to, in some sense, not only pray, but also to become the answer to prayer. In other words, never pray a prayer to which you are not willing to become the answer. We need to pray and get people to register to vote. If necessary, we need to write letters to Congress.
>
> Looking back at our history, we realize that we should have barraged our government leaders on every level when prayer was taken out of school. Our voices should have been heard without ceasing when it was made legal for babies to be killed in the womb. For many, we have been too passive in action while

decrying the decisions made at the top levels of our nation that in no way reflect who we are as a people. This is why we are determined to raise up an army of intercessors who both pray and act...There is nothing we could not see changed through praying and acting. We have this challenge before us: Will the U.S. become that shining city set on a hill that our forefathers dreamed of or will we lose our redemptive collective destiny?[12]

So, where are all the old-school intercessors? Are you one of them? Is God tugging on your heart to intercede for revival, to stand in the gap for your nation, to pray for your pastor? Intercession is a labor of love—God's love. I am calling for Spirit-empowered intercessors to rise up in this hour and take their posts—and take faith-inspired action. Churches, ministries, people, and nations need your prayers—and actions.

Chapter 13

HOPE ABIDES

For all the doom-and-gloom prophecies over America, there is yet a rising cry from respected voices from various streams of the body of Christ who sense God's heart—and hope—for America even in the midst of discipline. Despite the reality that a degree of judgment has come to America—and that we may continue to reap the wicked seeds we've sown for some time—many agree that God is not done with America. There is hope.

Mind you, it's not just voices from the prophetic movement who are decreeing and declaring hope for America. Evangelicals are rising up with words of confidence in God's desire to heal our land. Word of faith preachers are proclaiming that He has heard our prayers. These voices are growing louder than the doom-and-gloomers who are cursing our nation with their words—and they are building faith in the masses that God will visit us once again.

"If God can birth a nation in a day, He can change a nation when it strays. Of course, this is linked to our covenant relationship with Him," writes Chuck Pierce, president of Glory of Zion International Ministries and vice president of Global Harvest Ministries, in *Releasing the Prophetic Destiny of a Nation*. "Isaiah also says that nations are as a drop in the bucket to the Lord. Nations are no more diffi-cult to deal with than individuals."[1]

Despite this truth, hardly a day passes that Franklin Graham, son of evangelist Billy Graham, doesn't hear someone say, "We are losing our country; we are losing our churches." While doomsday appears to be knocking at our door, Graham points back to the early 1800s with words of hope that strengthen our hearts. "Many think of it as 'the good old days,' but history tells us that society, even then, was as bad as it could get at that time," Graham says. "John Marshall, chief justice of the United States Supreme Court, wrote to President James Madison and said, 'The church is too far gone ever to be redeemed.' When we examine why, we find that preachers had stopped preaching the whole Gospel of Jesus Christ, and the people were not hearing God's Word."[2]

"What changed?" Graham asked. Christians, he says, began to diligently pray for revival. The result was the Second Great Awakening.

"When people's prayers stormed the heavens, and when the Bible was opened in the pulpits and the Word of God proclaimed by passionate preachers, the church was awak-ened from slumber by the Holy Spirit, who moved in hearts, spreading revival throughout the heartland of America," Graham says. "There have been several Great Awakenings in our nation's history. When I read about them, I always go back to the Old Testament, to a time in which Israel had once again turned its back on God. When its people came to their senses, they gathered and asked Ezra the scribe to bring the Word of the Lord to them. The Bible tells us that Ezra stood upon a pulpit of wood, and he opened the book in the sight of all the people."[3]

The Alarm Clock of Heaven

Tim Sheets—author and pastor of Oasis Church in Middletown, Ohio, and Dutch Sheets's brother—has a heart for awakening and reformation in America. He says the alarm clock of heaven is now ringing on the nightstand of a sleeping church, and it's time to rise, time to rise to the occasion, time to get up! Consider this encouraging prophetic word he believes the Lord spoke to his heart:

> Great revival fire will now begin to burn through intercession-soaked regions as My awakening begins to roll. The regions will now become activated by My glory. My shaking has come. I am shaking earth. I am shaking heaven. Walls, strongholds, obstacles, and hell's defenses are being shaken down, and My remnant is being shaken free. My shaking will open ancient wells of revival. The revival in the womb of My intercessors will now be birthed.
>
> The revivalist mantle is descending upon My righteous evangelists. The fire shut up in their bones will now become words of fiery passion. With My gospel, I will shake open the capped wells of evangelism. I will shake open the ancient healing wells. Miracles will multiply. My angels are pumping those wells and they are opening new wells, new roads, new inroads, new mantles, new vision, new harvest. Behold I will do a new thing, and you will see it. Now it will spring forth.
>
> Because your cries have come before Me, because you have pursued My Presence…because your worship has become sweet savor—the Lord of angel armies decrees over His remnant people, you shall now begin reality church—no more acting, no more actors, no more pretending. Real church, real disciples, real

Christianity, real worship, real power, real glory, real miracles, real healings. It is ordained reality church.

I am now removing arrows shot into My royal priesthood. Arrows of betrayal, arrows of Jezebel, arrows of Absalom, arrows of deceit and gossip borne by lying spirits, arrows shot by those bound by religious demons. I your God am removing arrows. You will be free. You will be healed. You will be restored, and you will be on fire with My Presence for I have said, "I will make My ministers a flame of fire." It is ordained; your place of pain shall now be gain, and where you reign you will rise and rule with Me.

I am now coming to My remnant. And I am now coming as Lord Sabaoth-Lord of Angel Armies. Because of alignment with My purpose, I will now align My hosts to assist aggressively. There is now a convergence of the angel armies and the church's prayer army into a divine coalition; the coalition of My willing; those who run to battle, not from it.

My earth and My heaven's armies will now challenge thrones of iniquity, thrones of idolatry, thrones of rebellion, thrones of witchcraft, thrones of humanism and antichrist dominions. Battalions are dispatched and await the decrees of My word through the saints to overthrow iniquitous thrones so My saints can sit with Me.

My greatest campaign on Earth is due. Decree it…Align your words with Mine, and angel forces shall align with you. Align with angel forces in your regions, and I will accelerate an alignment within your nation. Yes, revival is now. The harvest is now…Victory is now…Arise and pursue My cause. Arise and roar. Arise and fight. Arise and shine. Your light has come, and the glory of your God shines upon you."[4]

Our Privilege and Hope

Lou Engle, cofounder of TheCall solemn assemblies that call young adults into a lifestyle of radical prayer, fasting, holiness, and acts of justice, is hopeful. He's been praying for revival for thirty years, helped plant two churches, launched the pro-life ministry Bound4LIFE, and helped raise up the first Justice House of Prayer in Washington, DC, to pray for the Supreme Court and for righteous leaders in America. After decades in the trenches of prayer, he's hopeful for our nation.

"[Fourteen] years ago, God opened a great door for a prayer revolution in America," Engle says. "That revolution, among other movements, was TheCall. Hundreds of thousands of men and women have gathered together in fields, stadiums, and arenas, to fast and pray, and have carried the flame wherever they have returned....Now, many look at the state of the nation and are deeply discouraged, but I am filled with hope. I have read history; most great moves of God erupted in the darkest times of crisis and were preceded by years of intercession. Today, I have more expectation for the Great Awakening in America than I ever have had."[5]

Francis Frangipane is the founding director of In Christ's Image Training, an online ministry school with students in nearly 115 nations, and author of books such as *The Three Battlegrounds* and *Holiness, Truth, and the Presence of God*. He asks two key questions: In the midst of terror attacks, blatant rebellion, and worldwide conflicts, is there yet one more great awakening in God's heart that will sweep multitudes into His kingdom? Or is the future irreversibly clocked, ever ticking toward catastrophic conflicts and doom?

"I, for one, am convinced that the Lord's heart burns for the nations," Frangipane says. "I believe that a great harvest season awaits us. It is easy to see sin and predict doom. Yet, the very fact that God gives us the privilege of prayer tells us He desires we participate with Him in the transformation of our world.

"Indeed, even when a nation seems fully in the grip of evil, the heart of God is searching for one who would 'stand in the gap before [Him] for the land.' God's heart is to redeem, 'not destroy' (Ezek. 22:30). What a tremendous insight into the nature of God, that if just one person embraces Christlike transformation—if he or she stands in the gap in unoffendable intercession—that individual can alter the future of a nation!"[6]

And Rick Joyner, founder and executive director of MorningStar Ministries and Heritage International Ministries and author of more than forty books, including *The Final Quest*, sees the enemy's plan clearly but remains hopeful for another transforming revival in America. "There are many great signs of revival and awakening in America— incredible things happening," says Joyner. "I believe we're going to see a Third Great Awakening in America within the next couple of years. It's going to be massive. It's going to transform America. It could help restore us to the foundations."[7]

"Hear God's Words, America"

As I mentioned previously, these words of hope are coming from many movements, not just from within the prophetic movement. Author and Bible teacher Kenneth Copeland released a dramatic prophetic word on November 4, 2014, that has inspired many. Here is the text of that prophecy:

The dominating power and authority of My WORD is very plain and very obvious in the Scripture. I made certain statements calling things that be not as though they were. I said a virgin would give birth to a child in the city of Bethlehem. And My WORD dominated the heavens and the earth and peoples in the earth for over 700 years until that child was born in Bethlehem at the appointed time, by the appointed virgin, and the Son came into the earth at the exact proper time.

I have spoken certain words over this nation. They will come to pass. They are coming to pass now... And all of the things that satan has attempted to carry out in order to stop My voice in the earth has come to naught. For I said this gospel of the Kingdom shall be preached in all nations and then the end shall come, and not before. It's coming to pass, and this nation is the cradle of that message. It has come out of this nation, the revelations and the changes that have taken place. And over the years and centuries that have gone by, I've called upon this nation to be My judgment arm. I've called on this nation to be My voice. I've called on this nation and many, many of your sons and daughters have answered My call and laid their lives on the line and I do not forget that.

So hear, My people. Hear My voice. Yes. The door is open. Repent and come through it; for I have a plan, and it's THE BLESSING plan, and it's far greater than anything you have ever seen before. I have a new birth for this nation. I have planned a nation that, right at this moment, you really don't have any concept of what it's like. For think back to 1770, 1771, 1772, 1773 and a new nation was being born.

But do you think that the men of that hour had any concept of what this nation would look like 100 years from that time? No. They had no idea. It had never happened before. Hear My words, America. I have a new nation in My heart and in My mind and you don't know what it looks like. The door is open. Step through it and together we will bring a new nation on the earth, one nation under God that trusts in God. And there are those that would say, "How could that possibly come to pass?" It can come to pass because I am God and I change not. And My plan has already been planned before the foundation of the world. And you listen to Me, and you walk with Me, and together we'll see it come to pass.

But for all of those who will turn their back on what I am doing now, you will be like those of old who get trapped in the desert, and your bones will fall in the desert, and you will not experience the greatness that I have in store. But I have a people. I have a people that have humbled themselves and have turned from their wicked ways, and I have more and more and more that are seeking My face. And I'll tell you this: I'm easy to find. And I've raised up people throughout this nation and I have a people all over this earth who are praying for the United States in this very hour, who are holding this country up before Me because they realize they need this nation also.

So these are the days of your deliverance. Rejoice, and be glad because I have given you your nation back. And the manifestation of its new birth is at hand. So rejoice and lift up your head and be of good cheer. Your sins are forgiven you.[8]

Riding the Fourth Wave

In the spring of 2011 James Goll had a vivid prophetic dream. In it John Wimber was the central figure, though this great Third Wave leader had graduated to his heavenly reward in 1997. Goll says three "waves" marked the twentieth century. Briefly stated, the first wave was the rise of the Pentecostal movement at the Azusa Street Revival. The second wave occurred during the 1960s in the charismatic movement. And the third wave came about in the mid-1980s and into the 1990s and was associated with leaders such as John Wimber of the Vineyard movement, C. Peter Wagner of the Church Growth Institute and Fuller Seminary, James Robison from the Baptist Fullness movement, along with many other significant voices of integrity with sound theology such as Dallas pastor Jack Deere.

In his dream, Goll says, the Holy Spirit used John Wimber to represent the Third Wave. He was told that the purpose for that movement had subsided and that it was time for another wave to roll in and make its mark on global church history. As he pressed into conversation with the Holy Spirit, Goll says God revealed to him that the previous waves included renewal, revival, empowering, and aspects of restoration—but a "fresh movement" was emerging on the world scene that would include all of the ingredients of the earlier movements because it was a time of the "Convergence of the Ages."

"I heard, 'It is time for the Fourth Wave to crash upon the course of history,'" Goll says. "This Fourth Wave would be one marked by transformation...The Fourth Wave emphasizes societal change by channeling these empowered believers to impact the seven cultural mountains of religion, government, education, business, family, media, and the arts and entertainment. Fresh intercessory strategies will now arise for effective ministry in the market place and beyond. The supernatural power of the Holy Spirit will not be able to be contained within the 'four walls of the church' but rather explode into every sphere of life. Apostolic hubs in numerous cities of the earth will emerge each with distinct assignments of influence releasing rippling supernatural effects into the different spheres of culture."[9]

Are you ready for the fourth wave? God is hearing our cries, but that doesn't mean we should stop pressing in now. In fact, I believe our level of desperation must increase before God breaks in and pours out His Spirit to bring a transforming revival. I believe we must continue making an appeal to heaven. And I believe as we do, it will transform our hearts and our minds to take part in the greatest awakening the world has ever seen.

"When the word of God is released through prophecy, it is never forgotten," Pierce says. "It is stored in heaven until God is ready to release it back into the earth. In the body of Christ, we have received many prophetic words, both through Scripture and through modern-day prophets, that are about to come to pass on the earth. We need to understand the times, seize our *kairos* opportunities, and move into the future with victory.

"Even though times ahead will change rapidly and may be difficult, we have great confidence that God will give us the revelation we need to move forward. When we are overwhelmed by our present circumstances and apparent defeats, we must hear the Lord speak to us, just as He did to Jeremiah, 'Is there anything too hard for Me?'"[10]

Conclusion

GOD IS NOT DONE WITH AMERICA

A DEMONIC TIDE of destruction has been unleashed upon our nation and is taking ground at an increasingly rapid rate. Politically, economically, and humanistically, there is an agenda to make this nation never again look the way it has looked before. Yet, God has not given up on America! He has great a plan and a purpose for this nation, and He is calling on us to partner with His heart and His strategy in this critical hour."[1]

So says author and Bible teacher Dutch Sheets, who travels extensively, empowering believers for passionate prayer and societal transformation. Dutch points to the Book of Ezra, which he says paints a picture of where America is today and shows God's desire to awaken, revive, and restore a nation whose God is the Lord.

Here's the scene: The children of Israel started rebuilding the temple after the consequences of their sin left it in rubble. "While they were hard at work, the people of the land—the enemies of God—discouraged the people of Judah, causing them to be filled with a paralyzing fear," Dutch says. "Counselors were also hired to work against the people of God and frustrate their strategy. This resulted in a sixteen-year delay in the rebuilding of the temple—the place, in that day, where God's presence and glory dwelled."[2]

In many ways, Dutch says, America currently finds itself in this sort of delay. After making great advances in kingdom building, many have let discouragement and fear gain a foothold in their hearts. "They've laid down their tools and folded their hands," Dutch says. "Others are busy with good kingdom works but don't dare challenge the status quo, much less the systems aimed at shredding the moral fabric of our nation, destroying the institution of the family, and stripping us of our religious freedoms."[3]

Indeed, it's easy to see how wicked counselors—in our days we call them lobbyists—are rising up to oppose God's people and advance an antichrist agenda in every sector of society. Dutch says this parallels the days of Ezra and fulfills the first three verses of Psalm 2: "Why do the nations rage, and the peoples plot in vain? The kings of the earth set themselves, and the rulers take counsel together, against the LORD and against His anointed, saying, 'Let us tear off their bonds and cast away their ropes from us.'"

Although these wicked counselors (or lobbyists) think they are succeeding, they probably haven't read the next few verses of Psalm 2:

> He who sits in the heavens laughs;
> the LORD ridicules them.
> Then He will speak to them in His wrath
> and terrify them in His burning anger:
> "I have installed My king
> on Zion, My holy hill."

> I will declare the decree of the LORD:

> He said to me, "You are My son;
>   this day have I begotten you.
> Ask of Me,
>   and I will give you the nations for your
>   inheritance,
>   and the ends of the earth for your possession.
> You will break them with a scepter of iron;
>   you will dash them in pieces like a potter's vessel."
>   —PSALM 2:4–9

"The good news is clearly laid out here—in the end, we win!" Dutch says. "Fellow warriors, we cannot fear that if we resist the government and the political activists, we might be taken out. Neither can we fear that we might go to jail, lose our government funding or tax-exempt status, or have our business shut down for speaking the truth or refusing to marry same-sex couples. Yes, these things are already happening—some are already paying a high price to stand for righteousness—but we cannot cower and live in a paralyzing fear. We must only move in the fear of the Lord."[4]

A Remnant Rising

Of course, the account from Ezra that Dutch shared is really only half the story. Dutch points out that God raised up a company of leaders who worked together to steer His people toward repentance and the restoration of the temple—after a sixteen-year delay. What moved God's heart? The people's hunger and desperation for God.

"First, God raised up two prophets, Haggai and Zechariah, to boldly awaken the people to their true condition, and to His desire for them," Dutch says. "The moment God's people responded in repentance, God began to work in their behalf. He frustrated the plans of the lobbyists and gave the people of Judah favor with the politicians. Everything they needed for the restoration of the temple was provided."[5]

From Dutch's perspective, the most amazing part of the story is how God's spokesmen (the prophets Haggai and Zechariah), God's government (the priest Joshua), and civil government (the governor Zerubbabel) came together to lead the people into reformation. In response to their obedience and righteous partnership, Dutch notes, the Lord blessed them by decreeing that the glory of the latter house would be greater than the former.

"Zechariah later prophesied to Zerubbabel saying [in essence], 'This mountain in front of you is going to be brought low and become a plain. Not by might or power but by My Spirit, you will tear it down with shouts of grace, grace!' This is a picture of what God wants to do in America!" Dutch says. "If the church wakes up from her slumber, heeds the voice of the prophets, and begins to partner with righteous government leaders to take her stand, the Lord will make a way for our nation's biblical foundations to be restored. His glory will fill our land once again. God's desire is that you would contend for and see revival in your city and nation!"[6]

Dutch also offers a sober warning: we cannot become so busy making money and building our own houses that we lay aside the often painful and sacrificial work of restoration required for God's kingdom to come and His will to be done in America. And yes, he says, it's OK to grieve over the condition of our nation, as Jeremiah or Nehemiah did. But he stresses that we must not give in to discouragement and fear.

"God is calling forth an army of faithful followers who will come up out of their discouragement to boldly push back the darkness," Dutch says. "Many leaders in government, health, education, and ministry are having to make a decision right now—am I going to make my stand or am I going to compromise and yield to the enemy's plans? I, for one, say what America's Founding Fathers said upon signing the Declaration of Independence and, thereby, committing an act of treason against the crown: I pledge my life, my fortune, my sacred honor—everything to stop this insidious plan of hell. Will you join me?"[7]

A Greater Great Awakening

I'm with Dutch. And I'm calling on intercessors and evangelists to partner in this hour to bring in the great harvest.

Julie Meyer, a worship leader at the International House of Prayer in Kansas City, sees God stirring His people to pray. She sees God raising up houses of prayer, prayer movements, and ministries that recognize the great need for prayer and for having foundations of intercession firmly established before ministry takes place.

"People are bowing their knee in reverence to our Holy God, believing that He gives more when we simply ask," Meyer says. "God set it up that way—that we would be co-laborers with Him, joining Jesus the Great Intercessor. We are simply to ask—knowing that God is listening and answering our simple prayers...The revivalists of old were men and women given to prayer. Before a Word was preached, the Heavens were stormed with prayers and petitions asking God to come, to act, and to move. *We are now entering a new era—for never before in history has God moved on the hearts of people worldwide with such an invitation to intercession.*"[8]

With that, Meyer shared a dream she had that she calls "A Great Greater Awakening." I'll step back and let Meyer share the dream in her own words:

> I heard a fresh cry exploding out of Heaven—an invitation for the nations to become part of the prayer movement that is blowing across the face of the earth like an unstoppable wave leading to a Great Greater Awakening.
>
> I was told in the dream to study and look back to the 1700s and the first Great Awakening—for this is our story. We are invited to say "yes" to prayer—we are invited to all become part of the story.
>
> I saw that many intercessors have grown weary and have become dull; therefore help from Heaven was sent to strengthen the heart of the intercessors, the prayer movements, and the houses of prayer that a glorious people would arise in unending prayers.
>
> We are in a Revelation 3:1–2 time frame, "I know your works, that you have a name that you are alive, but you are dead. Be watchful, and strengthen the things which remain..."
>
> God is inviting us to join His Son, the Great Intercessor, in prayer to birth His purposes on the earth. He is inviting us to be a part of the storyline of the ages. We are to be vigilant, to keep careful watch over His promises and purposes through intercession, to set our hearts toward Him, and to turn resolutely in the direction of agreement with His Heart for these days.
>
> I was in a deep sleep, and the dream started with the president of our Bible college singing an old hymn called, "I Love to Tell the Story." His voice was like a megaphone awakening my heart to the old, old story.

I had not heard this hymn in years since singing it as a young girl in the Methodist Church. He was wearing a blue suit and holding an old hymnal. His voice was loud. His voice was strong. He never stopped singing this old hymn throughout the entire dream.

As he was singing, these words and this melody awakened my heart all throughout the dream. It was as if the hymn was the backdrop to the entire dream.

Suddenly, I stepped into a scene where I saw seven ambulances all in a row with their lights flashing. They were lined up one in back of the other. There was great alarm in my spirit when my eyes beheld such a scene.

I noticed there were people on the sidewalk who were not that interested in the ambulances. Everyone was continuing to have their coffee and were talking— they were not looking at what was happening. People were just doing their thing and not bothered by the alarm that I felt in my body by the flashing lights. It was as if they did not even notice they were there. They were laughing and talking and having coffee, going about their day-to-day schedules.

I love to tell the story
'Twill be my theme in glory
To tell the old, old story
Of Jesus and His love.[9]

I went and looked in the first ambulance and heard the attendant say, "I cannot find a heartbeat," and I saw someone lying still on a gurney. I saw tiny, thin, and feeble legs. The attendant looked at me and said, "It's the intercessors. We are trying to revive the intercessors."

I looked in again, and it was as if the eyes of my heart were opened and I could see on the inside, and their hearts were failing. For the promises of Revival were so long in coming, it was as if the promises became too long to wait for and they were giving up and their hearts were failing. So I ran to the next ambulance, and the same thing was happening. I looked in and the attendant said, "I cannot find a heartbeat."

As I peered into the ambulance, I noticed that these attendants were not mere human beings; they were heavenly beings sent from the Throne of God. They were tall, they were large, and they were glowing as if lit from the inside with fire. Could these be the messengers of fire we find in Psalm 104:4? It gave my heart great hope to know that God has sent His angelic help to restart the hearts of the weary, the tired, the hopeless, and the feeble. These were the intercessors who have fallen asleep, those who have stopped contending because it became too long to contend.

Suddenly one of the attendants from the seventh ambulance at the end yelled, "I have a faint heartbeat, but it's dull." With those words, all the attendants leaned out of the back doors of the ambulances and they all shouted, "What did you do?"

The attendant in the last ambulance said, "Tell the old, old stories. For, as I began to tell the old, old stories, I found a faint heartbeat." So the attendants of the other ambulances began to tell the old, old stories, and I began to listen to these stories.

These stories went back to the 1700s. They began to talk about Count Zinzendorf and the Moravians, John Wesley, George Whitfield and Charles Spurgeon, and many others.

Suddenly the atmosphere was filled with shouts of, "I found a heartbeat, but it is dull." I ran to another ambulance, looked in, and this time I saw a faint movement. Suddenly this Heavenly attendant gave an order, like a command, saying: "Tell the old, old stories because the old, old stories are *your* storyline, they are *your* history, back as far as Count Zinzendorf and the Moravians, John Wesley, George Whitfield, Charles Spurgeon...

"For the baton was passed from generation to generation. The prayer movements of this day are the answer to the prayers of those in the great storyline of the ages. There is a timeline of Prayer Generals from generations past, and their prayer was that the Generals of prayer in 'these' days would arise; the prayer movement of 'these' days is the answer to their cries.

"You are in the storyline of the old, old story for their prayers begat your prayer. Put yourself in the timeline of the old, old story because the old, old, story—when told—will ignite the heart again.

"Though it will start as a dull beat, when *each* person will see themselves in the timeline of the old, old story, that dull heartbeat will begin to get stronger and stronger. For these are your ancestors—the prayer warriors of the ancient days—who lifted their cry for 'this day and this hour' that a people of prayer would arise in the earth to welcome back the King of kings."

Renewal in itself will not awaken dull hearts. But if you see yourself in the old, old story—the more you listen and put yourself in the history of the great storyline of prayer and revival—you will see yourself as the answer.

You are the continuation of their prayers. For the intercessors God is raising up today—the prayer movements in the earth today—are the answer to the prayers lifted up generations and generations ago taking us into the greatest awakening—the Great Greater Awakening.

These are your ancestors. You become the story, the plan, the answer, the revival for today—then you will never go back to dull hearts.

"Tell the old, old stories. Remember the old, old stories and see yourself in the storyline of Count Zinzendorf and the Moravians, John Wesley, George Whitfield and Charles Spurgeon, and many others who were great men and women of prayer—Charles Finney, Maria Woodworth-Etter, Smith Wigglesworth, Aimee Semple McPherson, Kathryn Kuhlman..."

You are *in* their story. Their history is *your* history, for you are the answer to their prayers: for a glorious and praying people, a shining and praying bride would arise in the earth who love prayer; and this cry of prayer will birth the Great Greater Awakening to welcome Him back.

I could still hear the song being sung:

I love to tell the story
'Twill be my theme in glory
To tell the old, old story
Of Jesus and His love.

It was almost as if I could hear prayers that were prayed centuries back—crying out for those who would take the baton to begin to cry out again until the coming of the Lord Jesus Christ.[10]

"You are a part of the story. We are a part of the story. It's almost as if we are the answer to the cries of prayer throughout the ages," Meyer says, "cries that said, 'Let a people who love prayer welcome Him back.' Let a praying people lift their voice for revival—let a billion souls come into the Kingdom. This is our story. This is our history. This is our season to take up the baton and pray, and then, watch revival spring up. We are in their storyline and they are in ours…This is our history and the joy of the journey ahead through prayer, and we put ourselves in the great storyline of the ages to welcome the Great Greater Awakening and to welcome Jesus the Coming King."[11]

Bishop Anne Gimenez, cofounder of the four-thousand-member Rock Church in Virginia Beach, Virginia, has been believing God for awakening in America for decades—and she's still believing. Through the years she and her late husband, Bishop John Gimenez, gathered hundreds of thousands of intercessors at meetings such as Washington for Jesus in the 1980s and 1990s and, more recently, America for Jesus in Philadelphia.

Here are her words of wisdom: "Only God knows what will happen next in America, but in my heart I believe we can see miracles as we call on God to heal our land," Gimenez says. "It's not about who's in the White House. It's not about our financial condition. It's about America turning back to God. America has started serving the gods of the people we conquered, just like Israel did. We're calling America to Jesus."[12]

Amen.

NOTES

Introduction
It's Time to Wake Up

1. As quoted in Warren Wiersbe, *The Wiersbe Bible Commentary: Old Testament* (Colorado Springs, CO: David C. Cook, 2007), 1310.

Chapter 1
The Spiritual State of the Union

1. White House, "President Barack Obama's State of the Union Address," January 28, 2014, http://www.whitehouse.gov/the-press-office/2014/01/28/president-barack-obamas-state-union-address (accessed December 1, 2014).

2. Ibid.

3. Ibid.

4. Legal Information Institute, Cornell University Law School, "Engel v. Vitale," http://www.law.cornell.edu/supremecourt/text/370/421 (accessed December 10, 2014).

5. David Barton, *America: To Pray or Not to Pray* (Aledo, TX: Wallbuilder Press, 1991), 11–12.

6. Ibid., 12.

7. CharismaNews.com, "Watch: Bold Cheerleaders Pray Despite Atheists' Threats and School Ban," September 19, 2014, http://www.charismanews.com/us/45475-watch-bold-cheerleaders-pray-despite-atheist-threats-and-school-ban (accessed December 1, 2014).

8. CBN News, "Victory Prayer Gets Football Coach Punished," September 25, 2014, http://www.cbn.com/cbnnews/us/2014/September/Victory-Prayer-Gets-School-Football-Coach-Punished/ (accessed December 1, 2014).

9. Kim Severson, "Mississippi Tells Public Schools to Develop Policies Allowing Prayers," *New York Times*, March 15, 2013, http://www.nytimes.com/2013/03/16/us/mississippi-requires-public

-schools-to-develop-policies-on-prayer.html (accessed December 10, 2014); Yahoo! News, "North Carolina Students Can Now Pray at School, Mention God in Assignments," June 25, 2014, http://news .yahoo.com/north-carolina-students-now-pray-school-mention -god-124806223.html (accessed December 10, 2014).

10. Guttmacher Institute, "Fact Sheet: Induced Abortion in the United States," July 2014, http://www.guttmacher.org/pubs/fb _induced_abortion.html (accessed December 10, 2014).

11. Ibid.

12. CNN Library, "Same-Sex Marriage Facts," November 24, 2014, http://www.cnn.com/2013/05/28/us/same-sex-marriage-fast -facts (accessed December 10, 2014). United Church of Christ, "About Us," http://www.ucc.org/about-us/ (accessed December 10, 2014); United Church of Christ, "GG9: Gay Games 2014," http:// www.ucc.org/gg9/ (accessed December 10, 2014).

13. Dana Ford, "Presbyterians Vote to Allow Same-Sex Marriage," June 25, 2014, http://www.cnn.com/2014/06/19/us/presbyterian -church-same-sex-marriage (accessed December 10, 2014).

14. Michael Paulson, "Methodists Reinstate Pastor, Deepening Church's Rift Over Gays," *New York Times*, June 24, 2014, http:// www.nytimes.com/2014/06/25/us/methodist-panel-reinstates -defrocked-pastor.html (accessed December 10, 2014).

15. Moravian Church in North America, "Moravian Church Northern Province Synod Approves Ordination of Gay and Lesbian Pastors," June 22, 2014, http://www.moravian.org/northern-province -synod-2014/moravian-church-northern-province-synod-approves -ordination-of-gay-and-lesbian-pastors/ (accessed December 10, 2014).

16. Adelle M. Banks, "Southern Baptist Leaders Cut Ties With California LGBT-Affirming Church," *Washington Post*, September 24, 2014, http://www.washingtonpost.com/national/religion/ southern-baptist-leaders-cut-ties-with-california-lgbt-affirming -church/2014/09/24/2aff2c46-4416-11e4-8042-aaff1640082e_story .html (accessed December 10, 2014).

17. *Daily Caller*, "Pedophilia Deserves Civil Rights, Says New York Times' Op Ed," October 6, 2014, http://dailycaller.com /2014/10/06/pedophilia-deserves-civil-rights-says-new-york-times -op-ed/ (accessed December 10, 2014).

18. Steve Hill, *Spiritual Avalanche* (Lake Mary, FL: Charisma House, 2013), 5–9.

19. Pew Research Religion and Public Life Project, "Public Sees Religion's Influence Waning," September 22, 2014, http://www .pewforum.org/2014/09/22/public-sees-religions-influence-waning -2/ (accessed December 10, 2014).

20. Jim Gaines, "One in Four Americans Want Their State to Secede From the U.S., but Why?", *Analysis and Opinion* (blog), Reuters.com, September 19, 2014, http://blogs.reuters.com/james rgaines/2014/09/19/one-in-four-americans-want-their-state-to -secede-from-the-u-s-but-why/ (accessed December 10, 2014).

21. Mike Huckabee, foreword to *God Less America*, by Todd Starnes (Lake Mary, FL: FrontLine, 2014).

22. Ibid.

23. Starnes, *God Less America*, 4.

24. D. James Kennedy, "America Adrift," http://www.djames kennedy.com/SitePlanner/Timeless%20PDFs/AMERICA%20 ADRIFT_DJK18812Z.pdf (accessed December 17, 2014).

25. Ben Carson, *One Nation* (Grand Rapids, MI: Zondervan, 2014), chapter 1.

26. Jonathan Cahn (Official Site) Facebook Page, transcript, "The Presidential Inaugural Prayer Breakfast," Keynote Address, January 21, 2013, https://www.facebook.com/notes/jonathan-cahn -official-site/the-following-is-the-transcript-of-the-key-note -address-jonathan-gave-at-the-pre/558000007557020 (accessed December 10, 2014).

27. Ibid.

28. Troy Anderson, "Billy Graham's 'Judgment' Letter Sparks Charismatic Commotion," CharismaNews.com, July 31, 2012, http://www.charismanews.com/us/33880-billy-grahams-judgment -letter-sparks-charismatic-commotion (accessed December 10, 2014).

29. Marcus Yoars, "America Shall Be Saved!", CharismaMag .com, September 1, 2013, http://www.charismamag.com/index.php/ component/content/article/18473 (accessed December 10, 2014).

CHAPTER 2
OUR EVERLASTING COVENANT GOD

1. In communication with the author.

2. Ibid.

3. Ibid.

4. United States Census Bureau, "State Area Measurements and Internal Point Coordinates," https://www.census.gov/geo/reference/state-area.html (accessed December 11, 2014).

5. Arthur Delaney, "Obama: U.S. 'Not a Christian Nation or a Jewish Nation or a Muslim Nation' (Video)," May 7, 2009, http://www.huffingtonpost.com/2009/04/06/obama-us-not-a-christian_n_183772.html (accessed December 11, 2014).

CHAPTER 3
OUR FIRST APPEAL TO HEAVEN

1. USHistory.org, "George Washington: The Commander in Chief," http://www.ushistory.org/valleyforge/washington/george2.html (accessed December 11, 2014).

2. George Washington, *The Writings of George Washington*, vol. 5, John C. Fitzpatrick, editor (Washington: Government Printing Office, 1932), 469.

3. History.com, "December 19, 1777: Washington Leads Troops Into Winter Quarters at Valley Forge," This Day in History, http://www.history.com/this-day-in-history/washington-leads-troops-into-winter-quarters-at-valley-forge (accessed December 11, 2014).

4. Ibid.

5. Eddie Hyatt, "George Washington's Unwavering Faith That Shaped America," CharismaMag.com, February 17, 2014, http://www.charismamag.com/life/holidays/19800-george-washington-s-unwavering-faith-that-shaped-america (accessed December 2, 2014). See also David Barton, America's Godly Heritage (Aledo, TX: Wallbuilders); "America's Godly Heritage 1," YouTube.com, https://www.youtube.com/watch?v=pme3o0WimkU (accessed December 11, 2014).

6. William J. Johnson, *George Washington, the Christian* (New York: Abingdon Press, 1919), 24–25.

7. Department of the Navy, Naval History and Heritage Command, "The U.S. Navy's First Jack," http://www.history.navy.mil/faqs/faq122-1.htm (accessed December 11, 2014).

8. Appeal to Heaven, LLC, "Welcome to Appeal to Heaven—the Story," http://www.ath.us.com/appeal-to-heaven-story (accessed December 17, 2014).

9. Department of the Navy, Naval History and Heritage Command, "The U.S. Navy's First Jack."

10. John Locke, "Second Treatise," The Founders' Constitution, University of Chicago Press, http://press-pubs.uchicago.edu/founders/documents/v1ch3s2.html (accessed December 2, 2014).

11. Perry Miller and Alan Hiemert, *The Great Awakening: Documents Illustrating the Crisis and Its Consequences* (n.p.: Bobbs-Merrill Educational Publishing, 1967).

12. Eddie Hyatt, "Christianity 101," The "Revive America" Project, May 8, 2013, http://biblicalawakening.blogspot.com/ /2013_05_08_archive.html (accessed December 2, 2014).

13. Eddie L. Hyatt, "Why We Must Recover America's Christian Heritage," CharismaNews.com, July 22, 2014, http://www.charisma news.com/opinion/44732-why-we-must-recover-america-s-christian -heritage (accessed December 2, 2014).

14. Daniel Webster, *The Speeches and Orations of Daniel Webster, With an Essay on Daniel Webster as a Master of English Style* (Boston: Little, Brown, and Company, 1914), 51. Viewed online at Google Books.

15. As quoted in Eric Patterson, *Politics in a Religious World: Building a Religiously Informed U.S. Foreign Policy* (New York: Continuum International Publishing Group, 2011), 41. Viewed online at Google Books.

16. As quoted in Robert C. Etheredge, *The American Challenge: Preserving the Greatness of America in the 21st Century* (Orinda, CA: MiraVista Press, 2011), 137.

17. *Church of the Holy Trinity v. United States*, 143 U.S. 57 (1862), viewed at Justia US Supreme Court, https://supreme.justia.com/cases/ federal/us/143/457/case.html (accessed December 11, 2014).

18. PewResearch Religion & Public Life Project, "Report 1: Religious Affiliation," Religious Landscape Survey, http://religions .pewforum.org/reports (accessed December 2, 2014).

CHAPTER 4
THE SYNERGY OF THE AGES

1. In communication with the author.

2. David Edwin Harrell, *All Things Are Possible* (Bloomington, IN: Indiana University Press, 1975), 6.

3. In communication with the author.

4. Gordon Lindsay, *Praying to Change the World*, vol. 1 (n.p.: Revival Library, 2014), "Introduction." Public domain.

5. In communication with the author.

6. Merriam-Webster.com, s.v. "synergy," http://www.merriam
-webster.com/dictionary/synergy (accessed December 17, 2014).

7. In communication with the author.

8. David Smithers, "Charles G. Finney," Awake and Go! Global
Prayer Network, http://www.watchword.org/index.php?option
=com_content&task=view&id=22 (accessed December 11, 2014).

9. American Studies at the University of Virginia, "Charles
Grandison Finney: 1792–1875," http://xroads.virginia.edu/~Hyper/
DETOC/religion/finney.html (accessed December 11, 2014).

10. Ibid.

11. Daniel Kolenda, "Prayer That Brings Heaven to Earth Part II,"
Christ for All Nations, January 6, 2012, http://us.cfan.org/bible
-study.aspx?id=10865 (accessed December 2, 2014).

12. As quoted by Jentezen Franklin, "The Ministry of Intercession," Jentezen Franklin Media Ministries, October 7, 2013, http://
www.jentezenfranklin.org/ministry-intercessory-prayer/ (accessed
December 2, 2014).

13. James G. K. McClure, *A Mighty Means of Usefulness: A Plea
for Intercessory Prayer* (Chicago: Fleming H. Revell Company,
1902), 26. Viewed online at Google Books.

14. Dutch Sheets's resources on the synergy of the ages, the
ancient path, and the appeal to heaven can be found at http://
dutchsheets.mybigcommerce.com/mp3/.

15. Jennifer Miskov, "There's a Tidal Wave of Revival on the
Horizon," CharismaNews.com, February 23, 2014, http://www
.charismanews.com/opinion/42887-there-s-a-tidal-wave-of-revival
-on-the-horizon (accessed December 2, 2014).

16. Ibid.

17. Ibid.

18. Ibid.

19. Ibid.

20. Ibid.

CHAPTER 5
GATHERING THE GENERATIONS

1. Shared in communication with the author.

CHAPTER 6
EVANGELISTS MOVE ON AMERICA

1. George Whitefield, *Sermons on Important Subjects* (London: Henry Fisher, Son, and P. Jackson, 1828), 151; *Christianity Today,* "George Whitefield," August 8, 2008, http://www.christianity today.com/ch/131christians/evangelistsandapologists/whitefield.html (accessed December 3, 2014).

2. William Thomas Ellis, *Billy Sunday, the Man and His Message* (Philadelphia: The John C. Winston Company, 1917), 292.

3. Barna Group, "Is Evangelism Going Out of Style?" December 18, 2013, https://www.barna.org/barna-update/faith-spirituality /648-is-evangelism-going-out-of-style#.VH81DtLF84I (accessed December 3, 2014).

4. Jennifer LeClaire, "Reinhard Bonnke: All America Shall Be Saved!" CharismaMag.com, February 4, 2013, http://www.charisma mag.com/spirit/evangelism-missions/16696-reinhard-bonnke-all -america-shall-be-saved (accessed December 3, 2014).

5. Reinhard Bonnke, "Raised from the Dead," ReinhardBonnke .com, http://reinhardbonnke.com (accessed December 3, 2014).

6. Yoars, "America Shall Be Saved!"

7. Jennifer LeClaire, "Reinhard Bonnke Searching for People Who 'Pray and Weep for the Salvation of America,'" CharismaNews.com, May 29, 2014, http://www.charismanews.com/ us/44022-reinhard-bonnke-searching-for-people-who-pray-and -weep-for-the-salvation-of-america (accessed December 3, 2014).

8. Shawn A. Akers, "Reinhard Bonnke: God 'Will Shake America,'" CharismaNews.com, September 27, 2013, http://www .charismanews.com/us/41172-reinhard-bonnke-god-will-shake -america (accessed December 3, 2014).

9. Ibid.

10. Ibid.

11. LeClaire, "Reinhard Bonnke Searching for People Who 'Pray and Weep for the Salvation of America.'"

12. Billy Graham, "Billy Graham: 'My Heart Aches for America,'" Billy Graham Evangelistic Association, July 19, 2012, http:// billygraham.org/story/billy-graham-my-heart-aches-for-america/ (accessed December 3, 2014).

13. Billy Graham, "Our Only Hope." Taken from "Return to the Bible" by Billy Graham © 1966 Billy Graham Evangelistic Association. Used with permission. All rights reserved.

14. American Bible Society and Barna Group, *The State of the Bible: 2014* (New York: American Bible Society, 2014), 23, 26, 11; PDF viewed at AmericanBible.org, http://www.americanbible.org/uploads/content/state-of-the-bible-data-analysis-american-bible-society-2014.pdf (accessed December 15, 2014).

15. Graham, "Our Only Hope."

16. Ibid.

17. Ibid.

18. Billy Graham, "Billy Graham: America Needs Our Prayers More Than Ever," Billy Graham Evangelistic Association, July 29, 2013, http://billygraham.org/story/billy-graham-america-needs-our-prayers-more-than-ever/ (accessed December 3, 2014).

19. Graham, "Billy Graham: 'My Heart Aches for America.'"

20. Harvest Ministries, "Harvest Crusades With Greg Laurie Celebrates 25 Years of Outreach in Southern California, Transforming Lives with Trademark Message of Hope," July 17, 2014, http://www.harvest.org/newsroom/article/harvest-celebrates-25-years.html (accessed December 3, 2014).

21. Greg Laurie, "Another Great Awakening in America?" *World Net Daily*, September 12, 2014, http://www.wnd.com/2014/09/another-great-awakening-in-america/ (accessed December 3, 2014). Used by permission.

22. Ibid.

23. Ibid.

24. Revival.com, "Souls," http://www.revival.com/souls/ (accessed December 17, 2014).

25. Adrienne S. Gaines, "Evangelist Says Revival Has Hit South Africa," CharismaMag.com, August 6, 2009, http://www.charismamag.com/site-archives/570-news/featured-news/6283-evangelist-says-revival-has-hit-south-africa (accessed December 3, 2014).

26. Revival.com, "Rodney Howard-Browne," http://www.revival.com/rodney-howard-browne.11.1.html (accessed December 17, 2014).

27. Gaines, "Evangelist Says Revival Has Hit South Africa."

28. *Ministry Today*, "Five Minutes With…Rodney Howard-Browne," MinistryTodayMag.com, http://ministrytodaymag.com/index.php/ministry-outreach/evangelism/16461-five-minutes-with-rodney-howard-browne (accessed December 3, 2014).

CHAPTER 7
TRANSFORMING REVIVAL IS TRULY POSSIBLE

1. Charles House, "Welcome Home," City of Manchester, Kentucky, http://www.cityofmanchesterkentucky.org/ (accessed December 15, 2014).

2. "Where Marijuana Is the Top Cash Crop," *Executive Intelligence Review* 18, no. 6 (February 8, 1991): http://www.larouchepub.com/eiw/public/1991/eirv18n06-19910208/eirv18n06-19910208_030-where_marijuana_is_the_top_cash.pdf (accessed December 15, 2014); Bernd Debusmann, "Residents of Appalachia Make the Transition From Moonshine to Pot," *Los Angeles Times*, June 30, 1991, http://articles.latimes.com/1991-06-30/news/mn-2473_1_marijuana-production (accessed December 15, 2014).

3. *Lexington Herald-Leader*, "Special Report: Prescription for Pain," January–February 2003, http://media.kentucky.com/smedia/2011/03/11/12/Drug_Reprint_Section_2.source.prod_affiliate.79.pdf (accessed December 15, 2014); Beth Smith, "Speaker Tells Officers How Churches Helped Town in Drug Spiral," CourierPress.com, May 19, 2011, http://www.courierpress.com/gleaner/news/speaker-tells-officers-how-churches-helped-town-dr (accessed December 15, 2014).

4. In communication with the author.

5. Ibid.

6. Wendy Griffith, "Town's Radical Change a 'Hope for America,'" CBNNews.com, October 22, 2010, http://www.cbn.com/cbnnews/us/2010/October/Appalachia-Towns-Transformation-a-Hope-for-America-/ (accessed December 15, 2014).

7. In communication with the author.

8. Sentinel Group, "The Fireplace," September 2013, http://www.sentinelgroup.org/category/transformed-communities/ (accessed December 15, 2014).

9. In communication with the author.

10. Ibid.

11. Ibid.

12. Ibid.

13. Ibid.

14. Ibid.

15. Ibid.

CHAPTER 8
OVERCOMING CHALLENGES TO
REVIVAL AND AWAKENING

1. Charles Finney, *Power From on High* (Fort Washington, PA: CLC Publications, 2005). Viewed online at Google Books.

2. Joseph Mattera, "13 Modern Challenges to Awakening and Revival," MinistryTodayMag.com, http://ministrytodaymag.com/index.php/ministry-news/kingdom-culture/20957-13-modern -challenges-to-awakening-and-revival?showall=&start=1 (accessed December 5, 2014).

3. Ibid.

4. The Apostles' Creed states: "I believe in God the Father, Almighty, Maker of heaven and earth: And in Jesus Christ, his only begotten Son, our Lord: Who was conceived by the Holy Ghost, born of the Virgin Mary: Suffered under Pontius Pilate; was crucified, dead and buried: He descended into hell: The third day he rose again from the dead: He ascended into heaven, and sits at the right hand of God the Father Almighty: From thence he shall come to judge the quick and the dead: I believe in the Holy Ghost: I believe in the holy catholic church: the communion of saints: The forgiveness of sins: The resurrection of the body: And the life ever-lasting. Amen." Viewed at "Apostles' Creed," Christian Classics Ethereal Library, https://www.ccel.org/creeds/apostles.creed.html (accessed December 16, 2014).

5. In communication with the author.

6. Ibid.

7. Ibid.

8. R. Loren Sandford, "A Fresh Move of the Spirit and a Warning," CharismaMag.com, http://www.charismamag.com/spirit/devotionals?view=article&id=19693:a-fresh-move-of-the -spirit-and-a-warning&catid=1567:prophetic-insight (accessed December 5, 2014).

9. Ibid.

10. Ibid.

11. Ibid.

12. David Ravenhill, "Are We Headed Toward Revival or Retribution?" CharismaNews.com, October 1, 2014, http://www.charisma news.com/opinion/45592-are-we-headed-toward-revival-or -retribution (accessed December 5, 2014).

13. In communication with the author.

14. Ibid.

15. Doug Stringer, "Revival Preparation Part 1," July 16, 2009, http://www.dougstringer.com/2009/07/16/revival-preparation-part-1/ (accessed December 5, 2014).

16. Ibid.

17. Ibid.

CHAPTER 9
REVIVAL PITFALLS TO AVOID LIKE THE PLAGUE

1. Michael L. Brown, *A Time for Holy Fire: Preparing the Way for Divine Visitation* (Concord, NC: FIRE Publishing, 2008), 19. Used by permission.

2. In communication with the author.

3. Charles Spurgeon, *The Sword and Trowel* (London: Passmore & Alabaster, Paternoster Row, 1866), 529, 533.

4. Gerard Couzens and Sara Malm, "Girl Aged 11 Has 104 Capsules Surgically Removed From Her Stomach After Becoming Colombia's Youngest Ever Drug Mule," *Daily Mail*, November 19, 2014, http://www.dailymail.co.uk/news/article-2840639/Girl-aged-11-104-capsules-surgically-removed-stomach-Columbia-s-youngest-drug-mule.html (accessed December 16, 2014).

5. Charles Finney, "Letters on Revival or Revival Fire," Christian Classics Ethereal Library, http://www.ccel.org/ccel/finney/fire/formats/fire.txt (accessed December 5, 2014).

6. Jonathan Edwards, *The Works of Jonathan Edwards* (Edinburgh: Banner of Truth, 1974), 1:398–404.

7. J. Lee Grady, "20/20 Hindsight: What I Hope We Learned From the Lakeland Revival," *Fire in My Bones* (blog), CharismaMag.com, December 3, 2008, http://www.charismamag.com/fireinmybones/Columns/120208.html (accessed December 5, 2014).

8. Brown, *A Time for Holy Fire*, 29.

9. Ibid., 63.

10. In communication with the author.

11. Ibid.

12. Ibid.

13. Ibid.

14. Ibid.

15. Brown, *A Time for Holy Fire*, 20.

CHAPTER 10
SUSTAINING REVIVAL UNTO REFORMATION

1. Joe Maxwell, "Is Laughing for the Lord Holy?", ChristianityToday.com, October 24, 1994, http://www.christianitytoday.com/ct/1994/october24/4tc078.html (accessed December 16, 2014).

2. In communication with the author.

3. Ibid.

4. Ibid.

5. Ibid.

6. Larry Sparks, "3 Keys to Sustaining Revival 20 Years After the Toronto Blessing," CharismaNews.com, January 20, 2014, http://www.charismanews.com/opinion/42478-3-keys-to-sustaining-revival-20-years-after-the-toronto-blessing (accessed December 16, 2014).

7. Ibid.

8. Ibid.

9. Larry Sparks, "3 Ways to Keep Revival Alive," CharismaMag.com, February 21, 2014, http://www.charismamag.com/spirit/revival/19833-3-ways-to-keep-revival-alive (accessed December 16, 2014).

10. Ibid.

11. Ibid.

12. Ibid.

13. Don Lynch, "Prophesy With Maturity: Personal Disciplines," October 31, 2014, https://drdonlynch.wordpress.com/tag/transformation/ (accessed December 5, 2014).

14. Adapted with permission from Lynch, "Prophesy With Maturity: Personal Disciplines."

15. Adapted with permission from Don Lynch, "The Forerunner Identity: Moving from Revival to Awakening Leadership," August 26, 2014, http://drdonlynch.wordpress.com/2014/08/26/the-forerunner-identity-moving-from-revival-to-awakening-leadership/ (accessed December 5, 2014).

16. Ibid.

17. Ibid.

18. In communication with the author.

19. Ibid.
20. Ibid.
21. Ibid.
22. Ibid.
23. Lynch, "The Forerunner Identity: Moving from Revival to Awakening Leadership."
24. Ibid.

CHAPTER 11
REVIVAL BEGINS WITH YOU

1. Michael L. Brown, "A Call to Personal Revival," CharismaMag.com, January 21, 2014, http://www.charismamag .com/spirit/revival/19618-a-call-to-personal-revival (accessed December 8, 2014).

2. A. W. Tozer, *The Pursuit of God* (Harrisburg, PA: Christian Publications, Inc., 1982).

3. Daniel K. Norris, "7 Signs You Need Revival," *From the Frontlines* (blog), CharismaNews.com, April 17, 2014, http://www .charismanews.com/opinion/from-the-frontlines/43539-7-signs-you -need-revival (accessed December 16, 2014).

4. Daniel K. Norris, "4 Ingredients in the Recipe for Revival," *From the Frontlines* (blog), CharismaNews.com, July 11, 2014, http://www.charismanews.com/opinion/from-the-frontlines/44614 -4-ingredients-in-the-recipe-for-revival (accessed December 8, 2014).

5. Bill Johnson, *Face to Face With God: The Ultimate Quest to Experience His Presence* (Lake Mary, FL: Charisma House, 2010), 2.

6. William Thomas Stead, editor, *The Review of Reviews*, vol. 31 (London: Mowbray House, 1905), 21.

7. *John G. Lake: Apostle to Africa*, complied by Gordon Lindsay (Dallas: Christ for the Nations, 1981), as quoted in Healing Rooms Ministries, "History of John G. Lake," http://healingrooms.com /index.php?page_id=422 (accessed December 16, 2014).

8. NewWorldEncyclopedia.org, s.v. "Charles Grandison Finney," http://www.newworldencyclopedia.org/entry/Charles_Grandison _Finney (accessed December 16, 2014).

9. William Francis Pringle Noble, *A Century of Gospel-work: A History of the Growth of Evangelical Religion in the United States* (Philadelphia, PA: H.C. Watts & Co., 1876), 317–319. Viewed online at Google Books.

10. Stanley Howard Frodsham, *Smith Wigglesworth: Apostle of Faith* (Springfield, MO: Gospel Publishing House, 1948), 44.

11. In communication with the author.

12. Mike Bickle, *Passion for Jesus* (Lake Mary, FL: Charisma House, 2007), 1.

13. Ibid.

14. Ibid., 4.

CHAPTER 12
MAKING AN APPEAL TO HEAVEN

1. As quoted in Trent Sheppard, *God on Campus: Sacred Causes & Global Effects* (Chicago: IVP Books, 2010), 161.

2. Anderson, "Billy Graham's 'Judgment' Letter Sparks Charismatic Commotion."

3. Ibid.

4. George Washington, "Thanksgiving Proclamation [New York, 3 October 1789]," Library of Congress, http://lcweb2.loc.gov/ammem/GW/gw004.html (accessed December 16, 2014).

5. William Pratney, in *The Revival Study Bible* (Singapore: Armour Publishing, 2010), 155.

6. Thomas á Kempis, "A Prayer for Cleansing of the Heart and for Heavenly Wisdom," in *The Imitation of Christ*, chapter 27. Viewed at Project Gutenberg, http://www.gutenberg.org/cache/epub/1653/pg1653.html (accessed December 8, 2014).

7. Jonathan Edwards, *Thoughts on the Revival of Religion in New England, A.D. 1740* (New York: American Tract Society, 1845), 106.

8. Charles Haddon Spurgeon, *Sermons Preached and Revised by C. H. Spurgeon, Sixth Series* (New York: Sheldon and Company, 1860), 25. Viewed online at Google Books.

9. Kenneth Copeland Ministries, "A Prayer for Revival," http://www.kcm.org.za/index.php?option=com_realhelp&task=article&id=260&Itemid=139 (accessed December 8, 2014).

10. National Day of Prayer, "National Prayer—Anne Graham Lotz," http://nationaldayofprayer.org/about/national-prayer-by-anne-graham-lotz/ (accessed December 8, 2014).

11. National Day of Prayer, "National Prayer by Greg Laurie," http://nationaldayofprayer.org/national-prayer-by-greg-laurie/ (accessed December 8, 2014).

12. Generals.org, http://www.generals.org/news/single-view/ article/prayer-activism-by-cindy-jacobs/. However, this article is no longer available online.

Chapter 13
Hope Abides

1. Dutch Sheets and Chuck Pierce, *Releasing the Prophetic Destiny of a Nation* (Shippensburg, PA: Destiny Image, 2011), 42.

2. Franklin Graham, "Franklin Graham: Praying for the Next Great Awakening." Taken from "Praying for the Next Great Awakening" by Franklin Graham © 2014 Billy Graham Evangelistic Association. Used with permission. All rights reserved.

3. Ibid.

4. Tim Sheets, "Great Revival Fire Will Now Begin to Burn," *Prophetic Insight* (blog), CharismaMag.com, September 23, 2014, http://www.charismamag.com/blogs/prophetic-insight/21372-great -revival-fire-will-now-begin-to-burn (accessed December 8, 2014).

5. Lou Engle, "My Prophetic Perspective After 12 Years of The-Call," TheCall.com, http://www.thecall.com/Articles/1000130456/ TheCall/CF/Prophetic_Perspective.aspx (accessed December 8, 2014).

6. Francis Frangipane, "The Last Great Harvest," http:// francisfrangipanemessages.blogspot.com/2011/09/the-last-great -harvest.html (accessed December 8, 2014).

7. Jennifer LeClaire, "Rick Joyner Predicts Destruction of Republic, Third Great Awakening," *Watchman on the Wall* (blog), CharismaNews.com, October 2, 2013, http://www.charismanews .com/opinion/watchman-on-the-wall/41218-rick-joyner-predicts -destruction-of-republic-third-great-awakening (accessed December 8, 2014).

8. Kenneth Copeland, "I Have Given You Your Nation Back," America Stands 2014 Broadcast, November 4, 2014, http://www .kcm.org.za/index.php?option=com_realhelp&task=article&id=82 6&sectiond=1&Itemid=139 (accessed December 8, 2014). Used by permission. Adapted with permission from James Goll, "When the Nation Is Thrown a Curve Ball," October 29, 2012, http://jamesgoll .blogspot.com/2012_10_01_archive.html (accessed December 8, 2014).

9. Sheets and Pierce, *Releasing the Prophetic Destiny of a Nation*, 61.

CONCLUSION
GOD IS NOT DONE WITH AMERICA

1. Adapted with permission from Dutch Sheets, "A Picture of America Through Ezra," September 10, 2013, http://www.dutchsheets.org/a-picture-of-america-through-ezra/ (accessed December 8, 2014).

2. Ibid.

3. Ibid.

4. Ibid.

5. Ibid.

6. Ibid.

7. Ibid.

8. Julie Meyer, "Julie Meyer: A Fresh Cry Exploding From Heaven 'I Love to Tell the Story,'" Elijah List, March 20, 2013, http://www.elijahlist.com/words/display_word/11961 (accessed December 8, 2014).

9. "I Love to Tell the Story" by A. Katherine Hankey. Public domain.

10. Meyer, "Julie Meyer: A Fresh Cry Exploding From Heaven 'I Love to Tell the Story.'" Used by permission from Julie Meyer.

11. Ibid.

12. Jennifer LeClaire, "America for Jesus Aims to Restore America's Foundation," CharismaNews.com, August 10, 2012, http://www.charismanews.com/us/33828-restoring-americas (accessed December 8, 2014).

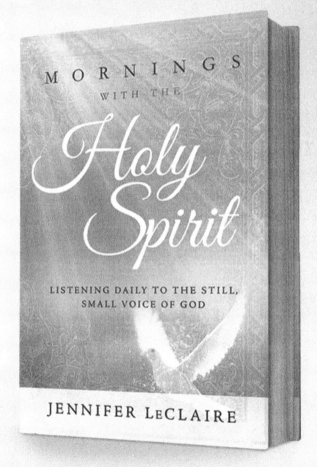